Credit Limits

Credit Limits

by
Joseph A. Weber
with Curtis Booraem, Ph.D.

Eight Fourteen Publishing
Santa Ana, California

Credit Limits

All rights reserved.
Copyright © 1996 Eight Fourteen Publishing

Reproduction in any manner, in whole or in part,
in English or in other languages, or otherwise
without written permission of the publisher is prohibited.

For information address: Eight Fourteen Publishing
3941-E So. Bristol St., Suite 346, Santa Ana, CA 92704
(714) 433-7185

PRINTING HISTORY
First Printing 1996

ISBN: 0-9655116-1-8
(Previously: 1-56901-852-9)

PRINTED IN THE UNITED STATES OF AMERICA.
10 9 8 7 6 5 4 3 2 1

To my wife, Pattie,
and our children, Robert and Anne Marie,
for whom my love has no limits.

Acknowledgments

My wife, Pattie, and our children, Robert and Anne Marie deserve a heartfelt thanks for granting me the time and space to write this book. They are my joy and inspiration in this life.

My sister, Helen Schleckser, gets a most special nod for her hard work in putting my scrawlings into manuscript form. My brother, Ed Weber, gets my thanks not only for his clerical work on this book, but his day to day assistance in my law practice.

Thanks to Natasha Shuqum for her prompt and professionally done research for this work.

Thanks to all the people who took time out of their busy lives to comment for the book, especially Dr. Curt Booraem for his analysis and insight. I want to thank my office staff—Danielle Gumbrecht, Christine Fredrickson, Bob Abui, Donna Winford, Megan Michael, and Chuck Finn for their extra efforts and support during the writing and production of this work.

Most of all, thanks to the thousands of clients I have had the honor of working with over the years. In sharing their pain and aspirations, perhaps I have become a better person.

CREDIT LIMITS

Most Americans over the age of fifty remember daily life without credit cards. Routine purchases were made by cash or check. Vast numbers of Americans still engaged in barter for consumer goods. Most of the time, those not in business only used credit for major purchases like a home, car, or large appliance.

In 1949, Alfred Bloomingdale, Frank McNamara, and Ralph Snyder formed Diner's Club. Though retail, gasoline, and even airline cards existed at this time, Diner's Club was unique in that it was to be accepted at many places of business instead of just one. In 1958, American Express and Carte Blanche enter this "universal card" field.

In those days, most charge customers received a bill at the end of the month which was all due and payable. Card companies and retailers soon realized that if the account was paid in installments they could make money far in excess of the profit on the original purchase through finance charges. The profit would be multiplied as repayment was extended; finance charges on universal and retail cards soon became common.

All over the country banks began issuing universal cards. In the 1960s, bank cards proliferated through the growth of multistate systems such as Bankamericard in the West and Mastercharge in the East. Well-financed and extensive marketing was to put these cards in the hands of tens of millions of average Americans.

By 1970 bank card use topped 7 billion dollars. Never before had this country seen so many credit cards in the hands of so many people. Formerly the privilege of only the well-to-do, credit cards were now available to anyone with a reasonable income. Accepted for all types of goods and services, including meals and vacations, every card holder now had "leverage"—purchasing power beyond the present ability to write a check. Instead of living from paycheck to paycheck, the consumer could now "increase" his present income to borrow against it and use it before actually earning it.

Banks were happy because they began making substantial profits on these operations. Merchants were happy because they could see potential sales increases. Consumers were the happiest of all because they could now extend the present buying power of their future earnings.

Approximately 16 percent of U.S. families had a bank card in 1970, 38 percent had one in 1977, and in 1989 the percentage was 54 percent. Was this the beginning of economic democracy or the dawn of a financial debacle?

During the years 1960-1969 there were 1,695,416 bankruptcy filings in the United States, or 8.34 for every 1,000 people. For the years 1980-1989 there were 4,583,391 bankruptcy filings, or 18.12 for every 1,000 members of the population. Was the great expansion of bank cards during this period just a mere coincidence?

The 1980s have been termed the "decade of excess." During this period credit card proliferation expanded rapidly as issuers expanded their marketing programs. In 1980 there were 180 million bank cards in circulation. By 1990 there were 207 million. The average balance in 1990 was more than twice that of 10 years earlier.

With interest rates on most bank cards at 16-21 percent, and the prime rate in 1992-1993 standing at 6 percent, it is no wonder that banks would be eager to issue so many cards. Even with a default rate higher than that of any other type of loan, these operations were still very profitable. In 1993 when a typical certificate of deposit (CD) paid 3-4 percent, the typical credit card rate was still at 18 percent.

In November 1991, President George Bush publicly commented on high credit card interest rates. This caused an uproar in Congress and adversely affected the stock market. Bush backed off, the market stabilized, and little was said again on this subject.

It is relatively easy to sit back and compile statistics about credit card proliferation, interest rates, debt, and bankruptcy. What we might forget, however, is that all of the above concern real people—you, me, and our fellow citizens.

Since World War II this nation has undergone major changes in its attitude toward credit, and to personal debt in particular. Many volumes have been written about national debt and the gross national product. I submit that we have largely ignored the effects of personal indebtedness on this country's values, economic infrastructure, and financial future.

Among other things, a nation is a group of people within geographic boundaries united by common factors such as language, monetary system, and culture. When there are big changes in a number of these factors there will be a change in what the nation "is."

The changes written about here are more than philosophical: they are behavioral. People now act in relation to their money like never before. Though the concept of extending credit goes back to ancient man, technology has amplified certain behaviors to the point where they have created rapid changes in society, as evidenced by the state of our present culture.

To attempt to understand these changes and their effects,

we must look at what individual people are saying and doing. I have tried to provide a starting point for this process.

It has been said that failure leads to success. This concept, joined with my personal familiarity with bankruptcy, can be one such reference point.

PREFACE TO CLIENT PROFILES

In the course of my law practice I have represented thousands of "debtors," the people who file for bankruptcy. My practice focuses on the two types of consumer bankruptcy, Chapter 7 and Chapter 13, which refer to the sections of federal law dealing with bankruptcy.

In a Chapter 7, the person attempts to receive a "discharge" or "wipeout" of debt from the court. In Chapter 13, the filer proposes a plan to pay debts over a period of time, usually three years. This is accomplished by making monthly payments to a court trustee.

Most consumer cases are filed under Chapter 7. A consumer case is one where an individual, as opposed to a corporation, has filed, and the debts are primarily credit cards and other personal obligations.

After interviewing thousands of people who came to me for advice about their debt problems, different patterns began to emerge.

I soon realized that *all* types of people file for bankruptcy—rich, poor, blue-collar, professional, "WASP," minority, etc. I also realized that most people who get into debt trouble start out with the best intentions about paying their bills. At some point they become "insolvent" or unable to meet their obligations as they become due. They then begin to investigate whether bankruptcy is appropriate.

The bankruptcy laws have existed in the United States since the 1800s. They underwent a major overhaul in 1978. The volume of bankruptcies has greatly increased since 1985. As the recession that began in the '80s continues into the '90s, the number of consumer bankruptcies appears to be directly affected.

In the Central District of California, which includes Los Angeles, Orange County, and the "Inland Empire" sections of Southern California, more bankruptcies are filed than in any other demographically similar part of the United States. Attorneys such as myself have plenty of cases.

Each of the profiles which follows represents a composite of at least ten different, actual clients I have either consulted with or have represented. I changed names and personal characteristics in order to maintain confidentiality; however, the dialogues and situations actually occurred.

I have attempted to focus on consumer bankruptcy situations where credit cards were a substantial factor, in order to raise issues in the reader's mind regarding financial problems associated with credit cards.

There is no intent to put all blame for financial failure on either the people who file for bankruptcy or the institutions who grant the credit. Rather, the profiles are intended to be viewed as a glimpse of what happens in real life.

Also, I created these particular composites to illustrate the diversity of the people I have worked with. Ironically, many of these composites are less dramatic and less sensational than actual cases I have handled. Some of those cases are so unique that if I described them here, the client's expectation of absolute privacy would be invaded.

THE YOUNG ADULT

Alice's expression was one of mirth and confusion. As we began the interview I read conflict in her face and manner as her story began to unfold.

On one hand, it was evident that the gravity of her financial situation had begun to sink in. On the other hand, she displayed a combination "so-what" streak of childishness mixed with adolescent defiance.

At the ripe old age of twenty Alice had one gold bank card with a credit limit of $5,000, several department store cards each with credit limits of about $800, and one travel and entertainment card. Her cards were "maxed out." She had borrowed the maximum amount of credit allowed for each card and her outstanding, unsecured debt totaled about $10,000.

For the last few years Alice had maintained steady employment; first as a department store clerk and then as a secretary in a public accountant's office. Although her monthly income was $1,200, her living expenses were greater. In addition to her credit card payments, her monthly expenses included $200 for a car payment, $400 for her share of the rent, $150 for car insurance, and $100 for utilities.

"How did this happen?" I asked.

She smirked and said, "I guess I just got carried away. What can they do to me anyway?"

I explained that there is usually about three to four months of collection activity which includes phone calls and letters. Then, if satisfactory payment arrangements are not made, the lawsuits start coming. If a creditor obtains a judgment, up to 25 percent of wages can be garnished. For Alice, this would cut her income to the point where even rent and everyday living expenses could not be met. Her situation looked like a

Chapter 7.

Once I explained this option and its ramifications, she lost her composure and the arrogant smirk gave way to sobbing.

A few minutes later she had regained her composure and posed another question. "How soon can I obtain credit cards after bankruptcy?"

"It's possible in about two or three years after the debts have been discharged by the court. However, all financial obligations such as your car payment must be made on time with no late payments. There is no slack and there are no guarantees. A lender is not obligated to extend credit to you. But even though the credit bureaus will report the bankruptcy for ten years, it is possible to obtain bank and store cards again within two years."

Next I had questions. "In the future, what will you do to avoid getting in over your head again?" and, "Do you know how to prepare a budget?"

We discussed how to set up a budget using my own home budget as an example. I soon realized that she, like so many other people, had never put such a theory into practice. I then decided that learning to budget income and expenses should be required by the eighth grade.

THE SALESMAN

Bob and Barbara caught my eye immediately. Barbara wore an expensive outfit that looked like something right out of the latest fashion magazine. Her chestnut brown hair was long and stylishly cut, closely resembling that of one of the more famous news anchorwomen. She wore a single gold pendant, tasteful and of excellent quality. Scanning her face, which seemed to be in the mid-forties bracket, I wondered whether she had ever indulged in cosmetic surgery.

Bob's dark blue suit was obviously custom-tailored and put some of my best to shame. His Rolex watch sported the classic silver and gold Jubilee band and the face had several expensive gemstones on it.

Their story was one I was hearing more and more lately. Bob was a sales representative for a national chemical manufacturer. Throughout most of the eighties he had routinely earned well over $100,000 per year. However, due to the declining markets in recent years, he was barely raking in between $45,000–$50,000. Barbara didn't work. The home they owned in an exclusive area had about $20,000 left in equity. Their two, high-ticket imported cars were both leased. They had no savings, no investments, and over $100,000 in credit card debt.

Because Bob worked strictly on commission, his net income at this time fluctuated between $1,500 and $5,000 per month. Since their mortgage payment alone was close to $3,000, they were coming up short.

"How have you been able to maintain your credit card payments for so long?" I asked.

"Robbing Peter to pay Paul," Bob answered.

This was the third time in as many days that a potential client had used this phrase. What it means is this: a person has various lines of unsecured credit. Each month he receives a bill from each creditor for part of the balance owed on each account. He obtains a cash advance from an open account to satisfy the installment payment on a different one. He makes each monthly installment payment in this fashion. In doing so, however, the overall debt rises, since the finance charges assessed each month are greater than the balance decrease due to the installment payment. I've had clients who insist that they have kept this "float" going for several years. As the outstanding balances continue to rise, more and more of the monthly payment is going toward interest, not principal. Therefore, there is little likelihood the person will ever be out of debt.

The interesting side effect of this situation can be a credit bureau profile with a perfect payment history. Creditors then interpret this person to be an excellent credit risk and offer higher credit limits and/or new accounts with automatic approval. Thus, while the person is drowning from the effect of too much credit, he is thrown new "lifesavers"—additional credit lines.

After discussing various options with Bob and Barbara, they decided to file under Chapter 7.

THE INVESTOR

Steve struck me as an interesting individual. He was a gray-haired, bespeckled man in his mid-fifties. He worked as a supervisor in a manufacturing plant and lived in an average middle-class neighborhood with his wife and children. They had a home with a reasonable mortgage.

For the last few years, he had been investigating ways of earning additional income through investing. To finance this he obtained bank cards with total credit lines of $100,000, borrowed the full amount in cash advances, and proceeded to invest.

His investment choices were the worst possible; they were the kind you see advertised on the back pages of tabloids or matchbook covers.

Steve believed that these investments would pay off over time and didn't mind making the large monthly payments, which ate up half his take-home pay.

He mentioned that the home was furnished sparingly and

he had reasoned that they would buy additional furnishings later as the investments increased in value.

Within a year and a half these "investments" dwindled one by one until each was worthless. Steve had nothing left except a home with minimal equity, two ten-year-old cars, and all that debt.

He felt a moral obligation to repay the debt, regardless of the fact that his investments had disappeared. Prior to visiting my office, he had contacted a local credit counseling service which made arrangements with the banks to accept lower monthly payments and even lower or suspend interest on many of the accounts. This eased the cash burden, and if everything had gone according to plan, Steve and his wife would have been out of debt in six or seven years.

Unfortunately, as the recession of 1990 hit, Steve's wife lost her job. With the loss of $1,500 in monthly income for six months and no offers in sight, they came in to see me. They were unable to make monthly payments to the credit counseling service, they were being sued by two of the banks, and Chapter 7 was the only way out of this bad situation.

THE FINANCE COMPANY MAN

Since all finance companies suffer bankruptcy losses, all the finance companies in my area eventually end up listed in someone's bankruptcy on a routine basis.

As part of our service to a client, we confirm by telephone with the creditor that a person is actually our client, and state the date their case was filed with the court. Often the creditor will then complain that the client has taken advantage of them, and many times will resort to labeling the person a "dirtbag," "deadbeat," or worse.

Since the finance companies in my area all have aggressive collection procedures, we communicate daily and consider each other "the opposition" as the bankruptcy case proceeds.

It was surprising then, to meet up with Mike, who at the beginning of our interview announced he had come to see me with his debt problem because he had worked at one of the area finance companies and had heard that I knew my stuff.

Before I could ask the usual opening questions, Mike authoritatively took out two pieces of paper and a pile of cash from his briefcase and lined them up in a row on my desk. He pointed to the first paper. "Here's a list of all my debts. You'll note that they're all unsecured." I scanned the list and noted that it consisted of about $70,000 on ten bank cards, each with an average balance of $7,000.

He pointed to the second paper. "Here's a list of all my assets. You'll note that they're all exempt." (The term "exempt" refers to the assets the law allows a person to keep when they file under Chapter 7.)

Then he pointed to the stack of cash, all hundred dollar bills. "And here's your fee plus the court filing fee. I want to do a Chapter 7."

I quickly responded, "Let me tell you about the different kinds of bankruptcy and ask you some questions."

"No, I know everything I need to know. Will you take the case and file it in two days?"

I made several more attempts to obtain information from this potential client and, receiving none, then informed him that I was swamped with work and could not possibly prepare his case in two days as requested. At that point, Mike quickly got up, said goodbye, and I never heard from him again.

THE ENTREPRENEUR

Ron and Betty were both friendly looking people in their early 60s. Ron was clearly the talker. Betty rarely spoke a word during our interview. She mostly nodded in agreement as Ron told their story.

About three years ago they had owned a small retail store. It was one which specialized in low-priced, popular, "in vogue" items of the time. Soon, though, demand dried up and their sales rapidly decreased. They left town owing several hundred thousand dollars to banks and suppliers. The abandoned stock and fixtures were worth less than $50,000 at liquidation prices.

"Why did you just walk away?"

Ron held up his hand before I could finish. "We knew at that moment that our work there was finished and went to find a new opportunity in another location."

Looking at their list of bills I saw that, in addition to the old business debt, there was over $200,000 in straight consumer debt—department stores, finance companies, and bank cards. Most of the consumer debt had been incurred after their involvement in the store had ended.

"How did you get all these credit cards after the business folded?" I wanted to know.

Ron answered, "Most of our accounts were opened before we closed the business and the new ones were easy to get."

"But how did you do it?" I asked again.

"Never mind, son," he admonished. "Will you take my case?"

Again, because of the potential for discharge threatening problems with creditors and because of my heavy workload, I had to decline.

THE ARTIST

Gene was an artist. He sailed into my office and I knew by his sighs of impatience that he'd rather be anywhere but in a lawyer's office.

Looking at the debt list of $25,000, I noticed that his debt was evenly divided between credit cards and personal loans from family and friends.

My first question was "How much money do you have coming in each month?"

He answered that it varied, depending on how much of his work was sold. Sales were slow now. A major show had just ended and although he had expected sales from this show to total enough for expenses for the next three months, he had earned only enough to pay living expenses for the next thirty days. Several of his credit cards were 60 days past due, bill collectors were beginning to call, friends and family were irate.

"I just want to declare bankruptcy on the credit cards, not the personal loans," he advised.

I patiently explained that in bankruptcy one can never choose which debts to list, the law requires that all must be listed. Of course, a person may pay anyone he desires *after* bankruptcy, but all present debt must be listed in the petition.

Gene was not happy with this information. "People will think I'm a flake!"

I counseled that the proper approach is to tell individuals about the bankruptcy *before* they receive an official notice from the court and to explain to them your intentions regarding future repayment.

"Go ahead and blame me," I told him. "Tell them that your lawyer is a stickler and insists on following the letter of the law."

The next problem was to determine whether his existing artwork could be "exempted"—was the liquidation value of these items low enough so that a bankruptcy trustee did not have to sell them and pay creditors with the proceeds.

Fortunately we were able to show by Gene's own estimate and through an independent appraisal that the artwork in his studio at the time of filing was indeed exempt. He kept it all.

THE DIVORCED MOM

"I haven't seen a dime of child support in three years!" Sharon cried. She further explained that if she had received the $300 per month in court-ordered support for her four-year-old son, she might have been able to pay down some of those "damn" bills.

Sharon worked in an office. Her take-home pay was about $1,600 per month. She rented a two-bedroom apartment for $800, her car payment was $220, utilities including the phone were $150, and monthly groceries were $300.

Her mom, a homemaker who lived in the same town, provided child care for her grandson at no charge. This was a lucky break, since the going rate for full-time child care averages $100 per week-per child.

Sharon had minimal assets but her credit card debt was over $12,000. She explained that most of the charges were for clothes, repairs on her five-year-old car, doctor bills and medicine not covered by insurance, and, lately, for groceries.

For the past six months she'd been "borrowing from Peter to pay Paul." She sells cosmetics out of her home for extra income, but sales had not been very good lately.

I asked, "Have you seen a family law attorney or talked to people at the district attorney's office about collecting some of your child support?"

"Yes," she replied, "but it doesn't do any good. He's up North working for his brother under the table. Whenever a letter is sent to the company they say he's been laid off or doesn't work there. And I don't have any money for a big investigation," she added.

"How about a part-time job?"

"I've put in about sixty applications," she replied. "No one's hiring."

"If we are able to get your debt discharged through bankruptcy, how will you make ends meet afterward?"

"I'll worry about that when it comes up."

THE WIDOW

Marion, a nice lady in her mid-sixties, sat across the desk. "My husband died last year after a short illness. He had no pension at work and the life insurance was just enough to cover the deductibles on his medical bills and to pay funeral expenses. I still have my job at the doctor's office, and with Social Security checks I'm netting about $2,000 a month. I only owe $7,000 on credit cards, but my rent is $700 and I come up short every month. By just making the minimum monthly payments, I can never seem to get out of debt. What can I do?"

This kind of situation is one where a "regular" or Chapter 7 bankruptcy is not a good idea. Why not?

The other type of consumer bankruptcy is the "Wage Earner Plan" of Chapter 13. If a person has money left over at the end of the month, regular income, and the desire to pay their debts, they can do just that through Chapter 13.

For Marion, this made the most sense. We were able to write a Chapter 13 plan where the creditors received full repayment, or 100 cents on the dollar, over a period of thirty-six months. Marion makes one monthly payment to the court trustee, who then distributes the funds to the creditors.

While the plan is in effect, creditors are under a court restraining order—they are not allowed to take collection action such as calls and letters. They are not allowed to institute or continue collection lawsuits, garnish wages, or seize property. Interest on the accounts, often up to 21 percent, stops when Chapter 13 is filed. All payments go toward principal, for the first time making it possible to get out of debt.

Another important feature is that when a person consolidates under Chapter 13, they retain the right to file a Chapter 7 in the future, should it become necessary.

Marion displayed both the ability and the desire to file a Chapter 13. In case of a disaster like a layoff or medical disability, she could always change her Chapter 13 case into a Chapter 7 and discharge the debts. Chapter 13 was her best alternative.

The reason many people with credit card debt always seem to stay in debt is the structure of the minimum payments. It is standard to see a minimum monthly payment of $50 on a $2,000 balance. Most of the payment goes toward interest, so it could easily take 10 years to pay off such a debt, if only minimum payments are made.

Many people either do not want to face this fact or are completely unaware of it. They stay on the plastic merry-go-round their entire working lives.

THE DOCTOR

It is widely believed that only uneducated or irresponsible

people file bankruptcy. This is not true. The vast majority of my cases are filed by people who regularly work and pay their bills. They either make a series of mistakes regarding money, or become a victim of a major setback or disaster.

Dr. Marshall is a good example of someone in the "mistake" category. He was in the third year of his own practice with a net annual income of $150,000. He had put himself through medical school and still owed over $100,000 in student loans.

In addition to large lease payments on his office equipment, he owed about $80,000 on bank cards which had been used to get start-up capital for his practice. Coupled with $1,500 per month for his mortgage payment, the bank card and student loan debts were eating capital as fast as it came in.

After a long analysis of assets we were able to show that Dr. Marshall could file Chapter 7, retain his practice, and obtain a discharge on the credit card debt. He was stuck with the student loans, though. In order to discharge student loans in Chapter 7, they must be *due* at least seven years. Any deferments must be added to the seven-year period.

Dr. Marshall was more than happy to continue paying on his education loans; "They got me to where I am today. I want the kids coming up through college to have the same opportunity I did. Hopefully, they will not repeat my mistakes with credit cards!"

THE GAMBLER

When one has large lines of unsecured credit, there is always the possibility that he will draw money out in cash advances and fall prey to vices like drugs, alcohol, and gambling.

Often I have seen people in debt who have used their remaining credit lines to try and gamble their way to solvency, in a last-ditch effort to "get even."

Jack presented his debt list, consisting of $10,000 on department store cards and $50,000 on bank cards. In the first few minutes he let me know that $40,000 of the bank card debt had been run up in the last two months, by taking cash advances and losing the money in Las Vegas casinos.

"What were you thinking?" I asked. Jack stopped staring at the floor and met my gaze.

"In the beginning I owed a lot to department stores and banks. I'm making these big payments every month and not getting anywhere, and then I get laid off. I'm getting $900 a month from unemployment and ten calls a day from bill collectors. Nobody's hiring and I'm starting to get antsy. After about a month of this I start doing afternoons at the track, taking a couple hundred bucks with me every day. I figure if I can win just $50 every time, I'm making just about what I was when I was working, if you add in the unemployment checks."

"So, what happened?" I asked.

"Everything was great for a few weeks—I'm hitting here and there, then giving some back. I'm pulling in a couple hundred bucks each week. Then I get greedy. I'm betting fifty, then a hundred bucks a day, and starting to get in the hole. Before I know it, I'm a couple of grand down."

The next phase of Jack's plan was to start making weekend trips to Las Vegas since the track had "gotten cold." He fell further and further behind, cash advances quickly piled up, and monthly bills with large minimum payments started coming in. It wasn't long before he sought me out.

At this point, it would have been a bad idea to file a Chapter 7 bankruptcy since the law would probably not help a gambler like Jack. In any bankruptcy case the creditor always has the right to contest the discharge of its debt. If a person takes cash advances of $500 or more shortly before filing bankruptcy and the creditor wants to contest, the creditor can start out with a legal presumption or "head start" in its favor.

I advised Jack to make monthly payments on the debt for as long as he could and then come back in six months or so.

I haven't heard from him yet—maybe he finally hit it big.

THE LAWYER

It is always a compliment when a fellow attorney seeks my advice, especially in regard to my chosen field of expertise—bankruptcy. I consider it even more of an honor when another attorney comes to see me about his own insolvency.

Many people, upon hearing this, have asked why an attorney like Charles doesn't just trot down to the law library and learn how to do the case himself. The reasons vary, but usually boil down to two things—the law and procedures change often, and most attorneys are too busy working in their own field to learn a whole new set of rules. Most attorneys are sharp enough to realize that there is an *art* to practicing law; a combination of knowledge, experience, and talent that simply can't be learned from a book.

Contrary to popular humor, attorneys are human and are subject to the same foibles as everyone else. Having handled about a dozen bankruptcies for other lawyers, I know this to be true.

Charles's situation was not very different from that of other small businesses. He practices injury law, and his income is derived from a percentage of the client's recovery after the case is completed. For anyone who has not watched daytime television in the last ten years, this is known as a "contingency fee," since it depends on the overall amount the client receives in the future. Cases like these often take a year or more to become resolved. In the meantime, the attorney has to advance expenses like filing and deposition fees and money for medical records and copies, in addition to the usual overhead of maintaining an office. If cases drag on before fees are received, a mounting financial burden can literally destroy a small practice.

This is exactly what happened to Charles. He was not able to resolve enough contingency cases to maintain the new ones coming in plus overhead. Virtually without income, he began "Robbing Peter to pay Paul": taking cash advances from bank cards to pay regular expenses like rent, food, and utilities. Soon he had passed the point of no return—the available credit lines were exhausted and there was not enough money coming in to cover expenses, let alone realize a profit.

Charles was able to obtain a discharge under Chapter 7, but it cost him his practice. He now works for a local legal clinic.

THE LOW-WAGE EARNER

Urban areas, like where I live and work, are diverse with respect to ethnicity and race. The vast majority of my clients are couples with children or divorced people with physical custody of a minor child or financial responsibility for the support and maintenance of a minor child.

I have represented many people who can be categorized as "working poor." Someone who is part of this group works at least forty hours per week, earns an average hourly rate of nine dollars, and struggles to raise a family and get by. This client is often male, rents where he resides, and has minimal assets, consisting of furnishings and a used car. His spouse works part-time or not at all. Many of these folks are first or second generation immigrants.

Unlike their higher wage-earning counterparts, these clients seem particularly vulnerable to consumer rip-offs and extremes in price and interest rates. Because of their limited earnings they are quickly hurt by escalating debt.

George was a ten-year U.S. resident and a brand-new U.S. citizen. He was employed as a waiter in a local restaurant. He had two department store cards with a total credit limit of $1,400 charged to $700, an appliance/stereo store card with $1,000 owed, and a furniture store account with a $1,200 balance. He had never obtained a bank card. George's six-year-old car took him to and from work in a reliable manner and there was no money owed on it.

Because George depends on tips, his income varies from week to week. His car insurance lapsed during one of these "slow periods." One night while on his way home after a particularly tiring night of work, he misjudged the distance between his car and the one in front of him while stopping at a red light. The person whose car he rear-ended developed back problems requiring $3,000 worth of medical treatment, in addition to the $2,000 in damage to her car.

Since George had no insurance, the victim's insurance company paid her medical bills and property damage and was soon suing George for over $10,000. While many insurance companies will accept monthly payments on this "subro" claim, this one was demanding more than George could afford—$200 per month. When added to his credit card debt payments of $175 per month, this $200 pushed him over the edge, since $375 is almost 25 percent of his take-home pay per month. A proud person who had been raised to avoid debt and always fulfill obligations, George immediately took a part-time job in order to meet these burdens. After only one month, his new job was eliminated and he was unable to find another. Facing wage garnishment from the insurance company, he decided to file a Chapter 7. Because the furniture and appliance accounts were secured debts where the creditor owns the collateral until it is paid for, George opted to keep making payments on those accounts in order to retain the items he had purchased.

Now George scrupulously pays his car insurance on time and says he will pay cash for all future purchases.

REAL PEOPLE

Several of my clients have been gracious and brave by writing their own account of how they came to file bankruptcy. I believe this has value to the reader because the situations presented are not filtered through me or seen from my side of the desk.

Bill & Pam M.

"You're preapproved for the Visa Gold Card. Consolidate all those high percentage cards to our lower-rate Gold Card and have a lower payment, too!"

We got so many offers like this for over twenty years. If we took them all, we probably would have had a $500,000 line of credit. Our problem was that we did accept some of the offers. After we consolidated all the cards to the lower rate card, the other cards were open for charging again. It was a never ending battle. Plus, all these cards were nice enough to give us checks so we could even use our credit to buy groceries if we were really short that week. But our credit rating was still "Triple A."

Then I was injured at work. Less income was coming into the household. When we were short money we would write a credit card check to cover the bills. The credit card companies loved us using the checks because you pay a fee to use them, plus 22 percent interest. Most of our payment was going to pay the interest on the accounts. That's when we began to start losing sleep and start fighting about money.

Then I began to write a credit card check out to pay one credit card and a check from that credit card to pay another. We were "robbing Peter to pay Paul" every month, just to keep our heads above water.

We own our own home. We thought since our credit rating was still good, we could easily get a home equity loan. We were turned down by one lender after another. We were told that our income was great, our credit was great, but our debt ratio was too high. I'd tell them that if you would let us consolidate, cut up all our charge cards, and even put a lien on our home, we would be all right. No one would take us, even finance companies that charge high interest rates. So I just kept writing out credit card checks every month to try and keep our heads above water.

Then someone (a loan officer at a bank, no less) told us about filing bankruptcy. I started calling phone numbers that were advertised on TV. I called numbers listed in the newspaper. Then a friend recommended our present attorney. We had to do something. We were both nervous wrecks and at each other's throats every time the issue of spending money came up, even for necessities. We couldn't file for bankruptcy. It wasn't right. We were brought up to believe that we had to be responsible for everything we did. When you're practically ready for a nervous breakdown, some things can fly out the window. After our counseling session with the attorney, we found out we weren't the only ones in this situation. Doctors, lawyers, movie directors, and people just like us file for bankruptcy. I still could not get over the guilt we experienced after our hearing. I knew we had incurred these debts, but we had a lot of help from the credit card companies. I wonder if besides checking credit histories to see if they are good, if they check to see how many credit cards a person already has. They make it easy for people in our society to have everything they want and to have it right now. After we filed and were discharged in Chapter 7, things got better for us; we had money to buy things. *Cash.* But, as part of the Chapter 7, we got to keep a few cards as long as we made the payments on them. As we went along, they even raised our credit limits. We were even reissued our American Express Gold Card plus a new Visa with a $2,000 line of credit.

I became disabled again before Christmas. It was real easy to charge things on the cards they let us keep. I was determined not to get into trouble again because I didn't think my nerves or my marriage could handle it again. I returned to work and I paid extra on these accounts because I knew we couldn't file again for six years. Things were going well.

Then Bill had a heart attack and triple bypass surgery. He received state disability benefits for six months. He was sick and recovering from surgery and our income was cut by almost $2,000 per month. If we had trouble before, then how were we going to manage now? Charge cards. That new Visa we got even had a PIN number so I could go to the ATM and get cash. That card bought most of our groceries and paid our utility bills. After all, state disability didn't even cover our monthly house payment of $1,200. Then to make matters worse, we had miscalculated our income taxes and owed almost $12,000 to Uncle Sam and to the State of California. These two government agencies have no compassion for anyone, even someone recovering from heart surgery. We were told we could make payments, but they still put a lien on our home. Our home was the only thing we had left. When figuring how much we had to pay each month, the IRS told us their average monthly allotment for charge cards was only

$200. If we owed more than that, too bad. They wanted their money.

I was ready to have a heart attack myself from all of this. Then my attorney told me we could file Chapter 13. Even though we had to make a monthly payment to the bankruptcy court each month, our debts were going to be paid and no one could make any judgments against us. The IRS even had to stop charging us interest.

We have been on the Chapter 13 plan for three years now and have two more to go. We didn't experience any guilt, since we are paying back what we owed. It feels like someone just gave us a big consolidation loan. The bankruptcy court is also willing to work with you. For instance, when your car breaks down or you need extensive dental work, they will suspend a payment or two until you are back on your feet.

All in all, bankruptcy can be a good thing. It can make you realize just what your obligations are. Yes, we did charge all that money, but we did have help from all the credit card companies.

Now we watch our children build good credit ratings. We worry about all the offers of credit they get. But they tell us, "Don't worry, we've learned from your experience." Oh, how I hope that is true!

Andy & Kathy B.

My husband Andy and I worked very hard at our jobs. He was a security guard. I was a waitress. Shortly after we were married we applied for and received our first credit card. I remember it well; it was a MasterCard. Somehow the name seems to have some grandiose meaning. We felt very important. After all, the credit card carrier did inform us that we were *preferred* customers. We never could figure out how we had achieved such status. One thing was for sure—we both knew that it was about time we received some recognition for all our hard work, and finally our reward had arrived.

After a couple of years of establishing good credit, we started receiving numerous offers for credit cards from different card carriers. Since we were managing our credit rather well, we decided that a few more cards such as gas and department store cards would make a nice addition; after all, they were so much more convenient to use than cash.

About three years into our marriage we had both changed professions. Andy went to truck driving school and landed a great job with the railroad. I earned my paralegal certificate and went to work for a major corporation.

During the next year we purchased our first home. While trying to finance the house we were informed that we would have to pay off all our credit card debts. Since we did not have the money to pay them off entirely, we borrowed approximately $5,000 from my parents to pay off the cards and an additional $15,000 for the down payment on our new home. We did not feel that we had overextended ourselves because we had both just received raises and it would be no problem paying these bills back. However, we made a decision to watch all our future credit card spending.

As we quickly moved up the ladder to success, we managed to purchase a brand-new truck and a car. We now had the American dream—a house with a pool, two new vehicles, a boat, and a camper. Of course, we also had a mortgage payment, car payments, boat payments, parent payments for the second mortgage on the house, and last but not least, credit card payments.

During this time, we managed to build ourselves an A+ credit rating. Almost every day we received a solicitation from some credit card carrier wanting us to use their particular card. We were no longer Preferred customers; we were now *gold*! We were proud of the fact that we were now pre-approved and all we had to do was sign and return the agreement.

In retrospect I think we associated charging and the use of credit with maturity and success. We were proud of our top-of-the-line cards; our preferred cards and gold cards. After all, they don't give credit to losers, do they? We felt great inside when we could just whip out our card and tell the clerk to charge it.

Before we knew it we had two MasterCards, two Visas, two Gold cards, two gas cards, and numerous department store credit cards. We were always interested when we would hear about a new card and wondered if we might have a need for that one, too.

We did not start out in debt. It began with a little charge here, another one there, and so on and so forth. We scarcely noticed it until it was out of control. For us, the process took about seven years.

We used to write a check or pay cash for most of the things we bought. Now we were charging most items on our credit cards. Keeping cards in reserve, we would bring a new one into play when we reached the maximum credit limit on the old one.

We were ignorant of the terms of our various loans, credit card agreements, and charge accounts. We never really did read the statements or knew what all the various figures meant. The most we knew about our credit arrangements was what the maximum credit limits were.

As our balances got higher we were only able to make minimum payments and could never seem to get caught up. It got to the point where it seemed as if we were working only to make enough to make minimum payments on credit cards. I must admit that we did have everything we wanted; however, that left us no margin for any new items we would later need or want.

Our bubble burst when Andy's job went out on strike. We used our entire savings account to stay afloat. We managed to get another gold card which we used for daily necessities until it was maxed-out five months later. We were struggling on only one income when I was informed that the wonderful job I had held for the last six years was forced into liquidation and in two more weeks I would be out of work.

At this point we were terrified that we would not be able to find new jobs and that we would lose everything we had worked so hard for. We felt ashamed and frustrated because we knew better than to let ourselves get into that much debt. We had to ask friends and relatives to loan us money. Knowing our circumstances, they were reluctant. It was so embarrassing.

Our creditors and their collectors were now calling us. We held off paying bills and told friends and creditors that we would pay them shortly. Whenever we could dig up some money to pay them with, we would. This would bring temporary relief, until next month.

Some of our creditors suggested that we contact a credit counseling center which would help us reduce our monthly bills and get us on our feet again. After reviewing our earnings vs. our bills, they informed us that we were bankrupt and suggested that we find a good bankruptcy attorney.

We took the counseling center's advice. When we contacted Joseph Weber we were three months in arrears on all of our bills and under tremendous pressure from the collectors. Joe was very understanding and sympathetic to our situation. We were reassured that even though we were filing for bankruptcy, we could keep our home, cars, and many furnishings as long as we continued making payments on them. We decided to file Chapter 7 bankruptcy and were able to keep all of our possessions.

Although we are not proud of it, the bankruptcy lifted a tremendous weight off our shoulders. It has allowed us to start over; only this time we're back to the cash and carry system.

We have both gone back to work and we are now learning to live within our means.

We laugh now, because even though we filed bankruptcy, we receive offers for credit cards from the very same carriers. They still say that we are preapproved and preferred. I guess you can be a loser and still get a credit card. Fortunately, we no longer feel like losers and are rebuilding our life and our credit profile.

Although we do not have any credit cards at this time, we can't say that we'll never have another card. We still live in a society that requires you to have credit in order to be recognized. We can only hope that this time we will be wiser where debt is concerned and not allow ourselves ever to get that deep into debt again.

Sally A.

I got into debt because it was so easy. I filled out credit applications at a few stores and received small credit limits. Making the monthly payments on time caused most stores to extend my credit when my balance got close to the limit. If I wanted to buy something that would go beyond my limit, it only took a phone call to raise it.

After I bought my condo I started receiving credit card offers with credit limits of $2,000 or more which only required my signature. They were so easy to accept. Most of these companies also increased my credit when I neared the limit. In addition, the same companies sent offers for other cards with the same credit limit. Now I had twice as much credit with each company.

When I started using the new credit cards and paying regularly, the "signature only" Gold Card offers began to arrive. These cards had credit limits of $5,000 or more. I accepted these offers too. It was hard to resist. The companies tell you that it's your outstanding credit rating which makes you so deserving of additional credit.

I don't understand why credit card companies give three cards to the same person. It appears as if they don't cross-check their files or calculate current usage. Some people (like me) shouldn't have too much credit.

With extensive credit, it was easier for me to spend money I didn't have. I used credit cards to pay for trips to the East Coast for weddings and funerals, car repairs, Christmas and birthday presents, and many impulsive purchases. I bought a computer and software (and more software), a video cassette recorder, television, and clothes. My old car began to fall apart so I bought a used car from a relative using a cash advance to pay for it.

I never worried about how deeply I was going into debt because I was making the required monthly payments. The security of a high-paying job and a condo which could be sold made it easier to ignore reality. I didn't consider the impact of the high interest rate and credit card insurance charges. Although I was making regular monthly payments, the outstanding balances didn't seem to decrease much.

When the layoff hit, I still didn't worry too much because I had credit insurance for unemployment and a condo I could sell. I put my condo on the market and received one low offer. The real estate market was deteriorating and I refused to give my condo away.

After seven months of unemployment the only job I could find paid less than half of my previous salary. When I accepted this job, the credit insurance companies stopped making the monthly payments on my accounts.

In about two months my phone was ringing every night. The collection process had begun. They were polite at first. Each wanted a promise of payment so I started getting cash advances from one to pay the other. Eventually my credit would run out and I would promise a smaller payment.

Whoever called first got paid. The calls became more threatening but did not violate the law. I finally began screening the calls because I couldn't deal with the collectors any longer. They prey upon people and harass them to the limit of the law.

I finally realized I had to do something so I called a credit counseling agency. They sent me an application and I scheduled an appointment. The weekend before my appointment I started filling out the application. It took a long time because I had so many debts.

After finishing the application, I felt I had "hit bottom," like alcoholics do. I looked at the amount I owed and was hit with shock, fear, and desperation which reached to the pit of my stomach. By the time I was interviewed by the agency, I already knew what they would conclude. I owed too much and earned too little for debt consolidation. The only solution was to file for bankruptcy.

The thought of bankruptcy scared me. I didn't know what to expect and was afraid of losing my home. The down payment had been made by a relative and I didn't want him to lose his money. I imagined a sheriff tacking a foreclosure notice on the door and carrying out all my possessions.

I made an appointment with an attorney a friend had recommended. He explained the bankruptcy procedure and relieved some of my fear. My equity in the condo did not exceed the bankruptcy limit since I was only half owner. I had no other assets, so the bankruptcy would be simple.

Once the bankruptcy was filed I had a case number to give to my creditors. For the first time in months I could answer the phone without worrying that it might be a creditor.

The day of my bankruptcy hearing I felt like I was the only person in the world who had filed for bankruptcy. I thought all my creditors would be there to challenge me. To my surprise the room was filled with people just like me. Two department store creditors were there but didn't participate in the hearing. Later I learned that they were there to attempt reaffirmation agreements with many other people besides me. This means that a debtor agrees to take back the debt with a smaller monthly payment. Full repayment restores credit with the store.

At the hearing I replied to a series of questions asked by the trustee. Then I left the room. Outside I declined on two of the three reaffirmation agreements. (I really needed the washing machine.) My attorney handled the negotiations so I didn't have to speak with any creditors. I went home feeling like I could finally get on with my life and decided that I could live without credit.

Now I am glad that I filed for bankruptcy. It forced me to live without utilizing credit and I have been successful so far.

THE SYSTEM

The bankruptcy trustee is the pivotal force in a consumer case. He or she is the person appointed to oversee the case for the court. In over 90 percent of consumer bankruptcy cases here, the debtor never sees a judge; only the trustee.

In a Chapter 7 the trustee examines the petition after it is filed and makes a preliminary assessment as to whether it will be an "asset" or a "no asset" case.

A no asset case is where the debtor gets to keep all his property as "exempt." An asset case is one where the person has property over and above what the law says he can keep after filing bankruptcy. It is the trustee's job to take these non-exempt assets, liquidate them, and use the money to pay creditors; usually at far less than 100 cents on the dollar.

In the Central District of California it is normal for a trustee to hold 40-50 hearings per hour over the course of a full day. The person is asked some standard questions: "Did you list all debts?" "Did you list all assets?" "Have you transferred any kind of property within the last year?" "Have you ever filed for bankruptcy before?"

Next the creditors are allowed to ask questions. Most hearings last no more than 60 seconds. The reason for such brevity is that the trustee has already reviewed the petition in which the debtor has answered over one hundred questions, and the debtor has signed the document under penalty of perjury.

The hearing becomes perfunctory—the trustee wants to see that the debtor is a flesh-and-blood person. The debtor must state for the record, again under penalty of perjury, that the answers given are accurate.

The fee paid to the trustee to administer a no asset case is small; about $45. Most trustees are attorneys, though this is not a requirement.

When a trustee administers an asset case the fee is about 3 percent of the money paid to creditors. For example, if the trustee administers $20,000, he or she may receive $600 after overhead expenses are paid. This compensation is governed by the applicable bankruptcy law.

Many trustees believe that such miniscule compensation, combined with a large caseload, makes their job uneconomical to perform. Also, it is almost impossible for them to adequately perform the main job Congress intended for this position: find hidden assets, uncover fraud, and ferret out debtors who have taken advantage of the system and bring to the attention of the authorities those who do not deserve a "fresh start" through bankruptcy.

One such trustee is Theodor Albert. A self-described conservative, Albert is deeply concerned by what he believes is a gross deterioration of personal accountability in the area of money. He believes that the generations born in this country after World War II are just "spoiled rotten."

"Too many people want their 'fair share' and feel that the system owes them. This attitude was seldom seen in our grandparents' time. Too many young people are too self-indulgent: spending money on toys like jet skis and living so far above their means that they don't know when to put the brakes on."

After acting as trustee for thousands of cases, Albert believes that there is a correlation between the role of government and personal responsibility. "People have to understand once and for all that there is no such thing as a free lunch. When someone wipes out debt in bankruptcy the rest of us pay for it in the higher cost of goods and services, including higher interest rates and fees.

"The government should set the example. It should cut budgets and costs throughout the system and do away with all the so-called 'entitlements' it hands out."

Albert believes that too many consumer bankruptcies are abusive. He feels there are many situations where the debtor has gone too far and may not be entitled to a fresh start. Albert suggests that Congress should amend the bankruptcy laws to include more repayment of debt.

"As things stand now, there is no incentive for a Chapter 7 trustee to deal with the current level of bankruptcy abuse I believe exists. Changes need to be made in the Bankruptcy Code; in its present form it actually *promotes* mischief."

Albert would like to see an "informed consumer movement" make a break from the present pattern by becoming better educated and motivated on financial issues. He maintains that demand for credit cards keeps interest rates high. He feels that more personal accountability should be sought, rather than "intervention by Big Brother."

"As a nation we must cease to borrow and buy more than we can afford. We have a tremendous populace in terms of raw talent; we have abundant natural resources, and a democratic system envied the world over."

• • •

Once filed, each bankruptcy case is assigned to a judge. Any proceedings such as a creditor's objection to discharge are handled formally in the courtroom by that judge.

In my area there are four bankruptcy judges. One of them, John J. Wilson, has been an attorney since 1954 and a bankruptcy judge since 1985. Unlike Theodor Albert, Judge Wilson describes himself as a political liberal, but many of his views are similar to Albert's.

"I am totally convinced that the expansion of credit cards, particularly those with cash advance capability, is the number-one cause for the great increase in bankruptcy filings over the last ten years," he says.

"My gut feeling is that 75-80 percent of all consumer bankruptcies have significant bank card debt. Of course, you need to remember that my view is very parochial—there are differences in what occurs in Biloxi, Mississippi vs. what occurs in Santa Ana, California and I have not conducted nor seen an extensive study on this issue."

Judge Wilson remembers a time when credit applications were more carefully screened. "In the sixties, while a partner in a major law firm, I had one or two department store cards and one or two gas credit cards. I applied for an account at a third store and was turned down only because I was separated from my first wife. Later we reconciled, but obtaining credit during the interim was almost impossible.

"Contrast that with some of the procedures used to grant credit today. I have heard of situations where a divorced person whose spouse declared bankruptcy couldn't obtain new credit for several years while a divorced mother with a few kids, nominal income, and still in Chapter 7 receives pre-approved credit card solicitations in the mail."

While Trustee Albert feels that bankruptcy laws should be amended to include more debt repayment, Judge Wilson has a different opinion:

"The proper statutes are already in place. Credit card institutions already have specific rights they can exercise if they feel abuse has taken place. These entities should be more aggressive in enforcing their rights. It appears that a certain percentage of all accounts are predestined to end up in bankruptcy and this percentage is factored into the procedure for granting credit. Most credit card companies write off debts which would be nondischargeable if the card issuer sought such a determination in the bankruptcy court. This encourages credit card abuse.

"Years ago when I was doing business workouts, we used a rule of thumb that a business which carried certain amounts of debt service at 15 percent or more could not survive more than six months."

On the question of whether people today are more responsible or less responsible with regard to personal finance, Judge Wilson says "less."

"People today live far beyond their means. They extend the repayment period for luxury purchases beyond the norm of three years. Thirty years ago I might have bought a decent suit for $100 and paid it off within six months. Now it is not unusual for someone to shop the mall with a few credit cards and spend four to five thousand dollars in one day. When this situation leads to bankruptcy, the credit card company says that tougher laws are needed. I find this offensive.

"If there must be revisions in the law, I would not be opposed to a statute that prohibits credit card solicitations prior to vigorous prescreening. A credit card should not be considered a commodity. It should be more difficult to obtain after bankruptcy. A fresh start should equal fresh responsibility."

Creditors of a person who has filed bankruptcy always have the right to object to either the entire discharge or the discharge of that creditor's debt.

The objection process is formal and done in the courtroom. An objecting creditor has its attorney file and pursue the appropriate action.

Gary Leibowitz, of the firm Leibowitz and Constantino, Tustin, CA, represents Sears for bankruptcies in my area. He has represented Sears and other creditors in thousands of cases, in addition to having represented thousands of debtors earlier in his career.

"Bank cards have always been a major cause of bankruptcy filings," he says.

"Fifteen years ago, the three major causes I saw were medical bills where there was little or no insurance, divorce, and misuse of credit cards. Now, it looks to me like 85 percent of consumer bankruptcies involve or are caused by overextension or intentional misuse of credit cards."

Like Trustee Albert, Leibowitz thinks bankruptcy laws should be changed. He says that the interpretation of the parts of the law dealing with nondischargeability of a debt vary too much between different judges. He suggests language like, "Reckless use of a credit card or charge account while insolvent shall render that debt nondischargeable."

Leibowitz is unhappy about the state of the bankruptcy courts: "The system is inaccessible because of too much bureaucracy and too many inconsistent procedural rules. Even a specialist needs a different set of rules for each courtroom."

On the issue of government regulation of credit grantors, Leibowitz believes "interference by government in the private sector almost always leads to disaster.

"No more than 10 percent of consumer bankruptcy cases involve substantial abuse, but in a dollars lost context, the numbers are staggering. Charging or taking cash advances on a credit card when the person knows they can never or will never pay back is just a type of theft, like shoplifting or embezzling. Better laws would put citizens on notice that this kind of behavior is just *theft* with appropriate penalties to be imposed."

Like our other colleagues, Leibowitz feels sure that people are much less responsible with their finances than in days past.

"Toys themselves are not the problem. It's this 'credit card mode' people get themselves into. Once they get going, they can't stop. It starts with restaurants and other entertainment on credit, then it's cash advances for rent and groceries.

"My father never had a credit card before I was in college. My father-in-law recently had to be shown how to use a credit card. They never incurred debt and would only spend what they had on hand.

"Families should teach and emphasize the practice of doing what is right or what is good. In a complex world it is all too easy to lose sight of basic values."

Consumer Credit Counseling Service (CCCS) is a non-profit organization started over 25 years ago to help those who got into debt over their heads.

The emphasis is on budgeting; counselors usually cut up the client's credit cards right before their eyes. It is not unusual for the client to cry or shake as this is being done.

In my area CCCS plays an important role. It has an excellent reputation as an alternative to bankruptcy and I will often refer people when I think there is a good chance they can avoid filing.

The CCCS program is similar to Chapter 13, except that it's not bankruptcy—monthly payments are made to the organization, which then distributes the money to creditors. Almost all banks and retailers accept what CCCS proposes. While they are often able to get interest on accounts lessened or suspended, the person's monthly payment is usually higher than in Chapter 13, since in the latter, unsecured creditors get zero interest on their balance.

Counselor Elizabeth Murphy, who has been with CCCS since 1988, says, "Consumers are using unsecured lines as an extension of their income. With the decline in many families' standard of living, unsecured lines and the proliferation of bank cards are truly a result rather than a symptom of our economic problems today.

"Credit grantors continue to extend credit in the same manner as they did twenty years ago, disregarding economic changes in the average consumer. Credit grantors approve or decline potential applicants with an 'assembly line' efficiency. How often do bank card centers verify title on a property or check year-to-date incomes? Many strong applicants fall victim to the point scoring system, whereas the weak applicant slides through.

"As a counselor, I see the consequences of prolific lending. After the first collection call, but before visiting the bankruptcy attorney, clients file in and out of CCCS offices nationwide in anticipation of making sense of their predicament. They don't understand why they are unable to live in the same manner as their parents. Their poor financial condition was a gradual climb. Each satisfactorily paid account brought new temptation for a 'better rate' or a higher credit limit. Even the smallest setback (i.e. new baby or new tire for the car) can begin the 'domino effect' that eventually leads them to my office."

Henry Sommer is co-manager of a neighborhood legal services office in Philadelphia, PA. He has been a lawyer for over 19 years, working in the field of consumer law the entire time. His work focuses on the problems of those with low incomes, which naturally leads him to do plenty of bankruptcy work. Sommer's typical client makes far less than the $18,000 per year cutoff for a family of four used by his office. Many of Sommer's clients receive AFDC or Social Security benefits.

His view on credit card proliferation is very straightforward: "The fact that there is so much credit card use is illustrative of the fact that banks are willing to take risks; poor people and the lower middle class pay the bulk of all high-end finance charges...They always have. I think banks are very conscious of this and just build in a certain default rate."

Sommer believes that increases in consumer debt are directly due to recessionary cycles. "When times are bad and consumers are carrying debt, they will have less money for goods and services because of interest payments they are already obligated to make. They will then borrow more if they can, which makes the situation worse."

But he does not believe that people today are less responsible than in times past: "There has not been that much of a change. Credit is just easier to get so there is more debt, but there is not necessarily a general decrease in personal responsibility."

When I asked Sommer if it was fair to equate credit card marketing, especially to young people, with drug dealing, he answered, "In some ways, but bad habits with credit cards are a lot easier to get rid of than drug dependencies. Both play to people's weaknesses or desires for a more glamorous, more pleasurable life."

On the issue of whether credit cards should be regulated like alcohol and tobacco, Sommer offered his opinion that legislation should be passed in all states that would prohibit *any* legal action to enforce a credit card debt. At first I thought he was joking, but once this concept was explained to me it began to make sense:

"Only a small percentage of credit card customers default—most people send in their payments each month," he explained. "Such legislation would put the risk on those most able to bear that risk—the banks. Creditors have too many 'levers' now. The wealthy and upper middle class have many ways to protect their assets, the low-wage earners have few assets to begin with, usually just their wages. Low-wage earners, being closer to the edge than other consumers, have always carried the system by paying most of its cost through interest charges. You or I are in a better position to pay off our credit cards at the end of the month, or obtain better interest rates when we have to borrow over time."

What would be the consequence to an individual who did not pay his credit card bills? "They would have their account canceled and be unable to obtain any new credit, which in this society would be the ultimate financial consequence," explains Sommer.

What about those who would get and run up large lines of credit with the intention of never paying?

Sommer answered, "Issuers would give this credit at their own risk. Their granting procedures would have to change. If such a situation did occur, the person would, in effect, be getting a 'Chapter 7 discharge in advance,' without actually filing. Of course, the number of bankruptcy filings nationwide would drastically decrease."

Frank Pees has been a Chapter 13 trustee since 1978, and administers more than 7,000 cases each year in the Southern District of Ohio, near Columbus.

"My average Chapter 13 debtor in 1979-1980 had a total debt package of $8,200 without mortgages and car loans, and paid that debt in around 42 months. Now it's around 19-22 thousand in consumer debt which requires 55-60 months to pay.

"Parents and other authority figures have the primary responsibility for making people aware of the pitfalls surrounding credit cards. Rather than having government regulate credit card promotion in print or TV, I look to the parents—if you think it's wrong, it's up to you to turn off the TV." Pees doesn't see credit card proliferation as some "sinister plot by the banks":

"Greed does not automatically equal profit. I saw a report where GMAC had something like a 50 percent default rate on one of its first-time buyer programs with certain dealers. I see a trend of people demanding and getting cards with lower percentage rates."

In 1986, Pees became frustrated with the inability of debtors who paid back their obligations through Chapter 13 and completed their plan to obtain new credit for everyday survival. He started his "Chapter 13 rehabilitation program" by sitting down with several local credit grantors and convincing them that the former debtors now deserved to have small lines of credit to meet basic needs—medical care not covered by insurance, clothes, and transportation.

"At first they were interested but aloof. I convinced them that their concern about increased bankruptcy filings was misplaced—if you can't control the filings maybe you can have an impact on the *type* of filing by recognizing what a person has accomplished by finishing their 13. I told them, to hell with Chapter 13 as the socially redeeming choice argument, people will always do what is in their best interest. If you make it tough on them to reestablish after 13 and they see their friends or neighbors driving a new car months after finishing their Chapter 7 and paying nobody that was unsecured, what do you think will happen?"

Pees's program now includes 44 grantors who have given over 22 million dollars in new credit to completed Chapter 13 plan debtors with a default rate of less than 1 percent. Chapter 13 trustees and creditors in other states have begun similar programs.

"Credit has become too impersonal," says Pees. "It's time to get back to talking with the lender face to face. It all goes back to communication. There are whole generations of kids now that were never really parented. Remember when 'day care' was just a safe reliable method for parents who needed to both work temporarily or a single parent to be able to work? Now it's a way of life. Does anyone except the truly naive really believe in the idea of 'quality time'? How can 45 minutes a day in some structured activity ever take the place of 4-5 hours in close proximity? If there is a problem later, I'm more inclined to blame a mushy-headed parent than an overgenerous or greedy creditor. It's true that we are in what I call the 'age of electronic capture,' but the parent can still control the remote."

Pees says we should remember the age-old question, "Whose values shall prevail?"

"We need to get back to the idea of more respect for the learned. Teachers are shot in the classroom now because the difference between right and wrong was not properly taught somewhere along the line. I tell my kids, don't use credit to keep up with the Joneses. Use education and preparation instead. You must be ready when the time comes."

TRENDS

Economists continue to argue over whether the latest recession is beginning, ending, or is over.

While the experts and politicians debate, Americans must still feed, clothe, and shelter themselves and their families each day. Businesses must continue to function and attempt to make a profit.

According to the Federal Reserve, consumers owed almost $729 billion in installment debt at the beginning of 1993, not counting real estate, including $324.4 billion to commercial banks, $112.7 billion to finance companies, $91.8 billion to credit unions, $40.7 billion to retailers, $33.8 billion to savings institutions, and $4.1 billion to gasoline companies.

This represents a continuing rise in revolving debt of more than a *billion* dollars every month.

It doesn't take many calculations to realize the tremendous amount of profit at stake in the credit card game. In 1993, bank card interest rates were in the high teens while a typical passbook account paid 4 percent. Banks get to use deposits to make profits of up to 18 percent over what they have to pay on this money. Naturally, they have plenty of dollars to spend on promotion for such programs.

Is "complaining" by credit card companies legitimate or just part of a program to make more profit?

In 1991 $3.5 billion was written off by card issuers because of personal bankruptcies, $2.25 billion in 1990, and $1.75 billion was lost in 1989.

In 1989, Visa started what it calls an "issuers clearing house" to help combat losses due to what it calls "fraudulent" or "abusive" bankruptcies. According to Visa's definition, this is a case where the person filing still has money left after normal living expenses to make a more substantial payment on debt. Visa has claimed that up to one-third of personal bankruptcies could fit into this category.

In my experience, I have found that different bankruptcy judges in adjoining courtrooms have very different views on what a "normal expense" is.

One judge may find $500 per month in groceries for a family of four "reasonable" while another might find this "offensive" and state a belief that $350 per month is more than enough. I have heard a judge refer to $100 per month spent on clothes for three people as acceptable while another believes $50 should be the limit.

Does this mean that bankruptcy judges are unsophisticated or completely out of touch with the real world? No. Just like the rest of us they are mere mortals; they are required to make decisions every day that are situational and relative to a certain set of facts.

When I hear a claim like "one-third of personal bankruptcies are abusive," I think of the thousands of cases I have handled and how defeated and embarrassed most of my clients appeared, and how the vast majority expressed, "I don't want to do this, but I can't pay my bills." This is the situation with well over 90 percent of the clients I have dealt with; it is doubtful that I am so poor a judge of people or mathematics that hundreds of "abusive" cases went by right under my nose.

Giving the credit card industry the benefit of all doubts, it would seem more logical that it has its own definition of "disposable income" and "reasonable living expenses." Would it surprise anyone to learn that such a definition is stricter than what people in the streets or practitioners in the field may believe?

In 1991, 70 percent of the money owed on credit cards was at 18 percent or higher, according to a study conducted for the Congressional Budget Office. In 1992 this fell to 44 percent. Why?

Part of the answer might be publicity from Congress itself. In 1991 there was a flurry of debate on credit card rates and even statements by President Bush to the effect that rates were too high.

Add to this the new credit card market entries from companies like General Motors and even H&R Block, which stiffened competition in a finite market.

In March of 1993, giant credit card issuer Citibank announced a new cardholder rate of under 14 percent. Norwest Corp. and Sears also dropped rates for certain customers.

In our information-rich society, as demand for something becomes known and established, there is usually someone willing to provide the item or service.

In May of 1993, a credit card guide called *Credit Cards USA* published by Ram Research Corp., was started. This newsletter publishes lists of cards with low rates or good benefits, and articles on consumer issues.

Organizations like FMP Financial Network and Bankcard Holders of America also publish lists of low interest rate cards. Perhaps an increase in such listings is the beginning of a new era in consumer awareness.

In such a competitive environment, great profits by credit card issuers can be quickly divided, resulting in less dollars for each institution.

February 1993 saw the advent of a new marketing campaign by MasterCard International with the slogan, "It's more than a credit card, it's smart money." One particularly poignant phrase used in one of the television commercials is "we're taking our MasterCard to the supermarket."

Have the materialistic '80s now evolved into the realistic '90s? In an era of recession and belt-tightening, do the credit card issuers recognize this and now wish to direct our buying on their cards to the more mundane?

Arguably so. Back when Diner's Club and American Express were two of few players on the block, one only used credit cards for the more exotic things—air travel, hotels, and restaurants. Now, credit cards are accepted at fast food places, convenience stores, and the regular grocery store. Consumers are apparently being pushed in this direction by the big guys. Perhaps their grand software has added up the *volume* of dollars in a competitive market and answered that "small is beautiful" and "mundane is more."

Before we all rush down to the 7-Eleven to take advantage of this new sophistication, it would be wise to spend a few minutes with the calculator. How much do those two six-packs end up costing if the purchase is carried on a bankcard for just 45 days? How much did they cost if that balance is carried for a year?

Now, using the same analysis, calculate how much $100 worth of groceries carried at 18 percent for one year ends up costing. With this kind of surcharge it makes no sense to "shop" if one is able to save fifty cents on an item but has to pay more in credit card finance charges over a certain time period. Under these circumstances there can be no savings.

When a business accepts credit cards, it is charged a fee by the issuer based on sales volume and sales amounts, which results in an added cost of 2-4 percent on each sale.

Merchants are divided on the advantages of accepting credit cards, usually depending on the type of business they are in. Low-average sale places like a video rental store will have a harder time than a furniture store, because of the lower profit margin.

Again, before we create new habits like using credit cards for smaller purchases we must consider how wide-scale spending for such items will affect prices in the long term.

Merchants are in business to make a profit. If billions of dollars in smaller purchases get made on credit cards and a point is reached where already low profit margins are eaten up, then prices will have to be raised in order for that business to survive.

We get it from two sides—one in higher cost through interest, and again in higher cost at the counter. This could create patterns that would end in a permanent drag on an already weak economy, much like barnacles on a ship, perhaps worse.

In March of 1993, tax preparer H&R Block announced it was offering its own card, the H&R Block MasterCard. For charging on the card, holders could earn a rebate on tax preparation services.

A company full of accountants must surely know how to

calculate potential profits available from issuing a credit card. Perhaps H&R Block will also institute a service warning its credit card customers when they are in debt over their heads. Perhaps a further discount toward tax preparation could be offered to customers who went bankrupt using the new card.

Other newcomers in credit card issuance include General Motors, AT&T, and General Electric.

Has American business deteriorated to the point where a company has to issue a credit card in order to make a profit, or was that point reached long ago? Or is the issue not one of just making a profit, but simply jumping on the bandwagon and making a much greater one?

Should the issuance of credit cards be restricted to large companies or should everyone, including sole proprietors and even families, strive to issue their own card?

"Hi, we're the Smiths, we're not home right now, but if you leave your name and number, we'll call you back. If you're calling about our current credit card rate, it's down to 12.5 percent this week. Don't forget that for every dollar you spend on our card we will credit you with twenty-five cents toward our next garage sale which is held every Sunday at 8 A.M...."

When it comes to the marketing of credit cards, truth and reality can be stranger than fiction and fantasy.

Just *weeks* after writing the above passages about a family issuing its own credit card, I received a letter from MBNA America Bank with my name—"Weber"—prominently printed at the top in big red letters. It started out, "Dear Weber family member: It is my pleasure to offer you a distinctive way to show your pride as a Weber...." It went on to announce "The Weber Family Card Visa," with special features like a low variable interest rate of 15.9 percent on purchases, an initial reduced rate of 12.9 percent on cash advances, two free gifts, no annual fee for the first year, and higher lines of credit.

Along with the letter came a nice color brochure showing two Visa cards, one black and one gold, with "Weber" printed boldly on each card.

This pitch was apparently designed to appeal to "family pride" as it centered around the history of my family name, one bonus gift being a research report on the Weber family name suitable for framing. Another bonus was a five-dollar gift certificate from the "one-of-its-kind catalog of heraldry," where I could get certain items with my family name and crest.

Unfortunately, the kind bank marketers never mentioned that in *my* family the "Weber name" was an anglicization of some unpronounceable Eastern European moniker.

Shortly after my father's father arrived at Ellis Island in 1915, he decided that his name should sound more American, hence "Weber."

While I might like to claim various privileges of heraldry, it could not be through the "Weber name." I had become a victim of well-intentioned mass marketing.

This was really okay, though, because I still felt good about myself after realizing that the people at the bank just wanted me to have an account there. The name business probably didn't matter much anyway, since credit is granted on one's financial status and payment history. I could still feel proud.

Should we look toward government to set an example? In 1991 credit card payments to federal agencies for goods and services approached $200 million. Many states accept credit cards for fines, taxes, and various user fees. Congress is considering legislation that will allow taxpayers to write in their Visa or MasterCard account information on tax returns and pay immediately.

Can it be long before governmental agencies start issuing their own cards? How about the "Deficit Reduction Gold Card"?

During hard times, it is all too easy to bash American business and government. There are those who believe the Japanese will be the world economic leaders in the 21st century. After all, aren't they more thrifty and hardworking than Americans? Don't they have a traditional culture that inhibits bad habits like overspending?

In 1987 Japan had 5 million Visa cardholders. In 1992 there were 37 million. Between 1987 and 1992, Japanese consumer debt topped $460 billion; an increase of 65 percent.

Interest rates for consumer loans are much higher in Japan than in this country; usually around 27 percent. Not surprisingly, personal bankruptcies in Japan have also risen.

As of June 1993, credit card issuers continued to grow. "Growth" is measured by the amount of money owed on the card.

Citibank led the group with $36.2 billion owed to it. Discover card, a relative latecomer in the field, was second with $17 billion, followed by MBNA America with $9.9 billion in receivables. According to Ram Research Corp., consumer debt increased by 3.95 percent among the top 10 credit card issuers during the first six months of 1993.

According to a July 1993 newspaper article, 71 percent of consumers do not pay off their credit card balances at the end of each month.

It's no wonder that so much is owed and the amounts seem to always increase. A weak economy coupled with aggressive marketing by banks must certainly be substantial factors.

In an August 1993 flyer sent to its customers, Bank of America loudly promoted its credit card: "From movie theaters to hospitals: Use your Bankamericard credit card wherever you go."

In this flyer, Bank of America informs that now grocery stores, movie theaters, fast-food restaurants, government agencies, and health care providers are accepting Visa and

MasterCard in growing numbers.

Can pay toilets that accept credit cards be far behind?

Economist John Kamin has published *The Forecaster* [19623 Ventura Blvd., Tarzana, CA 91356; $120 per year for 40 issues; 10 issue trial subscription, $39.] since 1962. He says that *The Forecaster* is really a "money letter" which gives his opinions about what *will* happen, as opposed to a "newsletter" which tells you what already happened.

Over the years Kamin has distilled his theories into "Kamin's Economic Laws." He points to his First Law as relevant to credit cards:

"All currencies will decrease in value and purchasing power over the long term, unless they are freely and fully convertible into gold, and that gold is traded freely without restrictions of any kind."

Kamin defines "Fiat Money" as that which only *represents* value, rather than having value in and of itself, or "intrinsically." He views printed currency not backed by gold or silver as fiat money. He considers credit cards to be a private form of fiat money, similar to currency that banks issued themselves in the 1800s. He mentions that Australia, which now issues $10 plastic currency, has experimented with plastic tokens to be used as "coins."

"I predict that credit card usage will triple within the next ten years," he says. This opinion is based on the premise that credit cards are too "well loved" by certain entities to not proliferate.

According to Kamin, *government* loves credit cards, mainly because they "keep no secrets"—purchases generated during a billing cycle and printed out on a statement give investigators plenty of clues about the user's personal habits; what kind of food they may prefer, where they have been, what type of clothes they wear, even with whom they have been associating.

"As credit card use increases, the cash or underground (not reported on tax returns) economy must decrease, another goal of government. Government on all levels also needs plenty of supporting documents and credit card records to simplify compilation. Such records simplify and standardize bookkeeping, as they will also provide proof that an expense was incurred, and preserve relevant details for tax deduction claims. Airlines may now report you to authorities as fitting a possible 'suspect profile' if you buy your plane ticket with cash instead of using a credit card or check!"

Kamin cites *banks* as another example of who loves credit cards: "A merchant pays 2 percent–6 percent to a credit card issuer in 'transaction charges' whenever it accepts a card instead of cash; banks make billions this way without ever seeing the merchandise or the services charged. Additionally, when a credit card is issued and then used, the customer is obtaining a loan for each transaction without the necessity of a loan interview or attendant paperwork. This increases the bank's overall profit on the loan since processing costs are reduced or eliminated.

"*Businesses* love credit cards," says Kamin. "When a customer uses a bank card, the financing overhead of the particular business is eliminated; the issuing bank has already approved the customer so the vendor does not have to. Paperwork is eliminated even more when the card issuer, rather than the business, sends a monthly installment billing statement to the customer. Bad check problems are diminished when a credit card is used—the credit card charge is approved or declined immediately. A check may be returned two weeks later, after the customer is long gone."

Kamin feels that accepting a credit card can also be used by a business to divert the customer's attention away from the price or quality of an item. He notes that most high-priced stores readily accept credit cards and theorizes that the *convenience* of charging, regardless of the high price, causes many consumers to purchase an item right then and there, rather than continuing to shop for a better price.

"Historically, I believe that 'Depression Babies,' like my parents, had an attitude toward money that was much different than what I see today. Either they paid cash or they didn't buy. In those days it was unheard of to refinance a house and take out money to use for 'whatever feels good.'"

Kamin recognizes a need for credit card management and sees more self-help organizations like Debtors Anonymous springing up as the 20th century ends. Like Ted Albert, he doesn't look to government to effectively regulate or set an example when "they can't control themselves."

"More courses with a better focus on credit management should be taught in high school and college. Responsibility should be taught *before* suffering and damage occurs. I've seen evidence that, depending on your definition of literacy, the national semi-illiteracy rate, defined as 'barely able to read and write or understand fine print,' may be as high as 40 percent. If accurate, this could result in a 'bonanza' for certain banks and businesses—we would see consumers continue to get loans without a new application and pay bills they do not completely understand.

"In the last half of the 1990s I see the emergence of more 'rebate' cards like the GM and AT&T cards, as well as more 'cash back' cards like Discover. I foresee more landlords putting an emphasis on credit card reports as a payment experience record for prospective tenants."

Kamin sees credit cards as a vehicle for the easy exchange of fluctuating currencies—"In the future I expect credit card usage in foreign countries to grow faster than in the U.S. In countries like Argentina or Poland, where the currency deteriorates within weeks, there can be great advantages gained by paying with plastic, since the bill is paid later and with cheaper money."

In October 1986, a case was filed in San Francisco Superior Court alleging that Bank of America conspired with Wells Fargo and other banks to fix credit card interest rates when Mastercharge made its debut in 1967.

The case, *Leary v. Wells Fargo Bank*, wound its way laboriously through the legal system until it finally went to jury trial in the latter half of 1993. Prior to that, defendants Wells Fargo Bank and First Interstate Bank settled for $55.1 million. Bank of America prevailed at trial, and was not liable for damages or found by the jury to have been part of any conspiracy.

The complaint alleged that California bank card finance charges had been artificially stabilized and maintained at noncompetitive levels; price competition for California bank credit card customers had been unreasonably and unlawfully restrained; and that California holders of credit cards from the defendant banks paid more in finance charges than if the alleged acts had not occurred.

A newspaper article in December 1993 quoted Visa as saying credit card purchases in 1993 were up 24 percent in department stores, 50 percent in mail order and phone purchases, and 76 percent in discount stores; all Visa purchases being up 28 percent over 1992.

In January 1994, Visa also announced it was issuing prepaid disposable credit cards on a trial basis. They expect to make the cards available nationwide by 1995. "Our goal is to replace cash and checks," a Visa spokesman was quoted as saying. "We want to be the preferred means of payment." The cards would be used like traveler's checks—purchased in certain denominations, but then used at ATMs to withdraw cash.

Another electronic trail for data gatherers to follow has now been created.

I asked my good friend, Curt Booraem, a clinical psychologist, to write about overspending and credit cards from the point of view of a professional working in this field.

The Psychology of Overspending
by Dr. Curt Booraem Ph.D.

Psychology is the study of human behavior. Like medicine, psychology recognizes the vast complexity of the human organism and as such has divided itself into many specialties. Clinical psychology, for example, is the study of abnormal behavior while consumer psychology is the study of behavior of the marketplace. It is important to distinguish between these specialties because each contribute differently to our understanding of problems associated with excessive spending.

For decades psychologists have been assisting manufacturers of consumer goods in product design, preferences, and marketing strategies. When products are developed to appeal to different sectors of the marketplace, psychologists frequently conduct the research to determine what appeals to whom. This includes studying differences in gender, race, age, ethnic background, and socioeconomic status. In short, psychology has contributed greatly to the materialistic preoccupation of American society.

Consumer psychology, however, must not be construed as all bad. Psychologists have also contributed greatly to product safety and consumer education.

Clinical psychologists become involved in yet another aspect of consumer behavior. When the consumption of anything reaches levels that are harmful to the individual, clinical psychologists are often sought to treat out-of-control behavior.

These behaviors are often labeled "Compulsive Disorders" and include alcoholism, drug addiction, gambling, kleptomania, pyromania, eating disorders, and compulsive buying. There are certain characteristics that are common to individuals with compulsive disorders.

The following pages will explore the roles of psychology in understanding specific factors related to increased consumption. In addition, we will explore the clinical manifestation of individuals at risk for compulsive buying and methods of treatment to reduce this risk.

CREDIT CARD PSYCHOLOGY

The advent of the credit card has led to a major expansion in product and service acquisition since its inception. It is generally believed by retailers, credit researchers, and popular writers that credit cards facilitate spending. Explanations of the relationship between credit cards and increased spending are generally economic and rational. Credit cards are seen as a convenient and rather painless way of spending. Consumer debt has become more socially acceptable and the use of credit cards lowers perceived cost of purchases and therefore begets further use.

Professors H. Lee Mathews and John W. Slocum Jr. from Penn State University, writing in the *Journal of Marketing*, described two general types of credit card users. Card holders who paid their balance within the billing cycle were considered to be using the card in lieu of cash, and therefore were referred to as *convenience users*. A card holder who elected to pay an amount less than the balance and pay interest charges on the unpaid balance was classified as an *installment user*. These authors went on to describe significant social class differences in credit card usage. Their data indicated that the percentage of installment use from upper class to lower class increases from 52 percent to 82 percent. An increase is also shown for each class progressively. Thus, members of different social classes exhibit different credit card use patterns. Members of the lower classes tend to use their credit cards for installment financing to a greater degree than the upper classes. The upper class is generally more favorable toward using credit to purchase luxury goods. Conversely, the lower classes restrict credit use to durable and necessity use. It also appears that the upper class's quest for distinction and achievement is a salient factor affecting their credit card philosophy.

Installment users who are predominantly members of the middle class and lower middle class have a favorable attitude toward credit and purchasing merchandise with the bank card and generally use their cards more than convenience users. The tendency to buy new appliances, furniture, and clothes on credit is somewhat more marked among those cardholders in the installment category than in the convenience user category.

The relevance of social class difference in credit card usage is important in predicting potential problems in credit overextension and insolvency. This is particularly true if consumers can be induced to increase credit card spending.

With this in mind, Richard Feinberg set out to determine if the possession of a credit card or cards increased the likelihood of spending. He also was interested in whether credit card symbols on signs advertising acceptance for purchases would also increase the frequency of credit card spending. In raising the question experimentally, Professor Feinberg considered the work of Leonard Berkowitz and his colleagues. Dr. Berkowitz was studying the stimulus control of aggression. Specifically, he questioned whether the presence of weapons in the home, school, workplace, or community would increase the likelihood of their use and also increase the frequency with which aggressive behavior occurred. The major finding of his research was that the presence of weapons triggered aggressive behavior.

Professor Feinberg reasoned that if the presence of weapons increased the frequency of aggression, then perhaps the presence of credit cards would increase spending. Pursuing this line of reasoning, Feinberg conducted a series of experiments with credit card signs and symbols. From these studies a number of important findings resulted.

Specifically, Feinberg demonstrated that the presence of credit card stimuli (MasterCard and Visa signs and symbols) increased the size of the tip left by credit card users in a restaurant setting compared to customers who paid cash. The experiment controlled for the size of the check and at each level the credit card user spent more money in the form of a larger tip.

In a follow-up study the individuals were given a list of consumer products and asked what they would be willing to pay for these products. One half of the people made their choices in the presence of Visa and MasterCard signs and symbols. The other half were not exposed to credit card stimuli. For each and every item on the list of consumer products the people exposed to the credit card stimuli indicated that they would be willing to pay more for the item than the individuals who did not see the credit card symbols.

Following up on this tendency for credit card users to spend more in the presence of credit card symbols, Feinberg wondered if the time it takes a consumer to make a decision about spending is also affected by symbols indicating that a credit card may be used in the purchase of merchandise or services.

In designing this experiment he evaluated college students individually, placing female students in a room with a slide screen mounted in front of them. Also on the table was a button labeled "response." The young women were told that consumer products would be projected on the screen in front of them and that they could look at the slide for as long as they wanted. They were told to press the response button as soon as they decided how much they were willing to spend on each object projected on the screen.

The women were divided into two groups as in the previous experiment. One group was exposed to credit card insignias and replicas of credit cards. The second group performed the same task but did not see the credit card stimuli. The results were even more dramatic. Not only did the women making decisions about purchases in the presence of credit card stimuli agree to spend more money on purchases than when there was no stimuli counterpart, but the amount of money they agreed to pay increased.

One could make the argument that these were college students and perhaps unsophisticated shoppers. However, women in the group without credit card stimuli were also college students and perhaps unsophisticated shoppers. Also, the prices they were willing to pay were grossly less than the credit card group. Take a look at the following examples: the credit card group was willing to pay $67.33 for a toaster, while the non-credit card group would pay only $21.50 for the same item. This difference is attributed entirely to the availability of instant credit. Consider a black and white television set. The credit card group would pay $136.92 while the non-credit card group would pay $67.00.

Try the purchase of a dress for comparison. The credit card group indicated that they would spend on the average of $49.42 while the non-credit card group would pay only $25.42 for exactly the same dress. How about an electric mixer? The credit card group said they would pay on the average of $36.25 for the mixer. The non-credit group again differed greatly—they were only willing to pay $17.75 for the same mixer.

These are outrageous differences in price for the same item. The only difference is the suggestion that you can charge it rather than pay cash immediately.

Now let's take this same study one step further as Professor Feinberg did. What about decision time? The credit card group required significantly less time to decide on the amount to spend. In almost all cases these rapid decisions of women presented with credit card stimuli led to a grossly increased price of purchase. The study found no difference between the groups in motivation to spend with credit cards. This means that each group was equally willing to use credit cards for these purchases. The outcome, therefore, of quick decision time to spend and increased price of purchase was due entirely to the effect of the symbols and insignias of credit cards to induce spending behavior.

In a final experiment Professor Feinberg questioned whether his findings regarding spending on consumer goods would generalize to charitable contributions. Again, testing college students for spending behavior in the presence of or absence of credit insignia, he found greater charitable contributions to the United Way in the presence of credit card stimuli. While the amounts contributed were low, it must be remembered that this was a college population. What is more significant is that 13 of 15 participants in the credit card stimuli group gave to the United Way, while only 5 of the 15 participants gave to the charity in the absence of credit card symbols.

How is it that the mere presence of a credit card in your purse or wallet increases your tendency to spend? Or even more subtly, the presence of credit card replicas or insignias prompts you to begin thinking about spending?

Psychologists have long believed that the reward associated with acquiring goods or services increases the likelihood of future spending. The person thinks consciously or subconsciously, If it feels this good, I'll do it again, more often and sooner. The spending behavior is, therefore, self-limited by the availability of funds. Credit by definition extends the reach of this form of reward or pleasure. Problems develop when the individuals with credit cannot or do not balance their need for reward or pleasure with the realities of their financial ability. The ability to exercise self-control over spending and indebtedness is very difficult for millions of people and is impossible for some. However, as if this weren't difficult enough, we now see from the work of Professor Feinberg and others that you can be provoked to use your credit card. We know that the act of carrying it with you increases the likelihood that you will use it. We also know that the mere presence of replicas or symbols of MasterCard, Visa, American Express, etc. is increasing the likelihood that you will spend. Worse yet, they provoke you into spending faster.

How is it that these symbols have so much power?

Their use is based on another form of learning psychologists call classical conditioning. That is when learning occurs by association, or by the pairing of events: stove-hot, snow-cold, money-spend. Leonard Berkowitz and his colleagues demonstrated that the presence of weapons increases violence. The studies I have just mentioned demonstrate that symbols of credit cards increase the frequency, amount, and decision time to spend. Classical conditioning of this sort is very subtle and works on the fringe of our awareness. How often do you notice the credit card symbols when you are in the marketplace? Sometimes you do and sometimes you don't. Most of the time you do not consciously look for them, yet they are there subtly exercising their power. Often you are aware of the symbols but do not record them consciously; other times your awareness is completely subconscious. On still other occasions you may have a memory, however vague, that this establishment accepts credit cards and the mere presence of the symbols validates the memory and creates a new mindset with an increased propensity to spend. The marketplace has a vested interest in your spending and this includes banks, finance companies, and other money lenders. They realize that a small percentage of consumers will become insolvent and declare bankruptcy. However, these losses are an acceptable risk to most business enterprises. The amount to be gained by enhancing sales no matter how it is done is worth an occasional reversal. With this in mind, all manner of promotional schemes are presented to you with the ultimate intention of getting your money, either now (cash) or later (credit). If the marketers can induce you to spend by working on your subconscious mind, they will. They will assault you with campaigns to convince you that you won't be likable, attractive, smart, popular, powerful, or any other desirable trait if you don't buy or use some product or service. The marketers will come at you directly or subliminally. They will praise you and they will insult you, all for the same end. Your best defense is to (1) buy time and do not buy impulsively and (2) make a decision in advance about your purchases and how much you are willing to spend on them. These two strategies will raise your consciousness to the act of spending and in so doing increase the likelihood that you will exercise more wisdom in the act of consumption.

THE PSYCHOLOGY OF COMPULSIVE BUYING

Here we will explore the characteristics of individuals who have little or no resistance to spending and who ultimately suffer greatly for this problem.

Compulsive buying may be viewed as part of a broader

category of compulsive consumptive behaviors. The American Psychiatric Association defines compulsions as repetitive and seemingly purposeful behaviors that are performed according to certain rules or in a stereotyped fashion. They are often excessive and ritualistic behaviors designed to alleviate tension, anxiety, or discomfort aroused by an obtrusive thought or obsession. In the strictest sense, compulsions are behaviors performed against the conscious will of the individual. However, the term is frequently used to classify a number of repetitive behaviors driven by an irresistible urge and ultimately harmful to the individual.

Compulsive consumption can take many forms. It would include drug and alcohol abuse, eating disorders, and compulsive sexuality. It would also include such marketplace-oriented behavior as kleptomania and compulsive gambling.

The labels used to describe these behavioral excesses are many. Consider the following terms: addictive, compulsive, excessive, habitual, abusive, impulsive. All these terms are used interchangeably by many media sources. However, despite this inconsistency in labeling, there is general agreement on the basic definition of compulsive disorders. The two essential criteria that must be present in these various disorders are (1) the behavior must be repetitive and (2) it must be problematic for the individual.

In the early stages of these problem behaviors the individual sees the difficulty. In fact, the behavioral excess generally reduces anxiety or makes the person feel good or better in some way. It is only after some period of time that the negative consequences accumulate and the individual begins to recognize they have a problem. The newly developed awareness of the problem may also be distressing and therefore prolong the difficulty.

You may wonder how compulsive buying relates to other, obviously more severe problems. After all, drug addiction, kleptomania, and pyromania are all criminal behaviors. How can compulsive buying be anything like these criminal acts? The similarities are in the origin, not in the act itself. They are also similar in that they are repetitive behaviors that are problematic for the individual.

It is also possible for people to engage in compulsive behaviors and manage their lives reasonably well. Ulysses S. Grant became an army general and the supreme commander of the Union Army during the Civil War and later became the eighteenth president of the United States while being a heavy drinker. One of the physicians who founded John Hopkins Medical Institute had a lifelong heroin addiction. During those times opiate use was not a crime. The doctor tried on various occasions to cure his addiction without success. Despite this failure he led a long and productive life which by all accounts was not affected by this compulsive disorder. Compulsive cigarette or cigar smokers are at much greater risk for cancer and heart disease while functioning normally in most other areas of their lives.

The issue here is that having a compulsive disorder does not necessarily make you a dysfunctional or bad person. It merely increases the likelihood that you will have difficulty functioning in some areas of your life. With some compulsive disorders there is a great deal of dysfunctional behavior and treatment is essential to restore normal functioning.

Now let's explore the phenomena of compulsive buying and some of the factors associated with its cause. By current estimates, fifteen million Americans are compulsive buyers. Women are more likely than men to be compulsive buyers. Depending on which studies you review, somewhere between 60 and 90 percent of compulsive buyers are women. There are three patterns of excessive buying: daily shoppers, binge shoppers and impulsive shoppers. Impulsive shoppers often experience remorse for their purchases but rarely get into big trouble. It's with daily shoppers and binge shoppers, that the compulsion has its greatest negative effect.

Compulsive shopping typically occurs in response to negative life events. Most compulsive buyers purchase things for themselves, but some buy almost exclusively for others. Some, but not all, compulsive buyers report that they make multiple purchases of the same item. And many people with this problem report that at least some of the items they purchased were not needed or were never used. Many compulsive buyers hide new purchases to avoid conflict with other family members. It is not uncommon for compulsive buyers to never even take a purchased item out of its packaging. Dr. Ronald Faber of the University of Minnesota, a well-known expert on compulsive buying, believes that items purchased by compulsive buyers may have "less meaning" than those purchased by regular buyers.

The products purchased by compulsive buyers are not random but instead fall into consistent groups of products. These include clothes, jewelry, makeup, electronic equipment, and collectibles. These items are often linked to self-esteem either through how one looks or how one thinks about one's self, i.e. collectors of art, etc. These types of purchases frequently involve positive interactions with salespersons which further enhance self-esteem.

In reviewing the work of Professor Faber we find there are a number of characteristics common to all compulsive buyers. These include the fact that the individual initially makes a voluntary decision to engage in an activity but eventually experiences urges to repeat the behavior that cannot be controlled. These behaviors often become a primary means of escaping stress or unpleasant situations. Typically, people experience repeated failure in attempts to stop or limit these behaviors, although the behavior begins to interfere with normal life functioning.

In trying to understand this extreme phenomenon psychologists have identified biological, psychological, and sociological factors that appear to contribute to the development of compulsive buying.

On the biological side some researchers believe there is a genetic element making people from families with some form of impulse control problem more at risk for these disorders. Studies of compulsive buyers have tended to find that people suffering from this problem are also likely to have other impulse control disorders. One of the neurotransmitters (serotin) has been linked to impulse control disorders and there has been some success in treating these problems pharmacologically. It should be pointed out, however, that success rates remain below 30 percent and that other personality factors contribute greatly to the problem.

On the psychological side, a number of personality factors have been associated with compulsive buying. As a group they have lower self-esteem than the general population and they have a much higher level of fantasy and imagination than average. Compulsive buyers tend to be less attached or interested in the objects of their purchases. They are much more involved in the process and interactions of buying than they are with the outcome. The average man who wants a new electronic product shops for one that pleases him most and that is within his budget. Once he makes his choice and purchases the item he takes pleasure setting up and operating the device. Hence, the reference "toy." The compulsive buyer is like a child: hungry for nurturance and affection. The act of acquiring the toy from the parent by whatever means is proof of their love. The fact that the child's room is filled with toys he never plays with is immaterial to his fundamental psychological need.

Compulsive buyers also tend to have little social support in their lives. They have few if any friends and poor family relationships. They may be shy or inhibited and otherwise lacking in social skills. They may feel self-conscious about themselves, which is consistent with their low self-esteem. Because of this they may describe sales people as their close friends. They frequent the same stores for social reinforcement and know the UPS driver and the mail carrier by their first names.

Sociologically compulsive buyers get unneeded reinforcement from our cultural environment. Shopping per se is not that bad. It wasn't too many years ago that most women shopped daily. Prior to refrigeration and food preservatives it was necessary to go to market frequently to obtain fresh meats, produce, and bakery goods. The process of gathering food has been a human task since the origin of the species. In tribal societies women gathered fruits, nuts, and berries and other edible plants while men hunted for meat sources and larger game that could sustain the tribal group for longer periods. Compulsive buying is an extension of normal behavior that is out of control. But it is inadvertently reinforced by society making light of it. Humorous accounts in the media serve the function of excusing and diminishing its destructive potential. Proclamations such as "Shop till you drop" and "When the going gets tough, the tough go shopping" create almost a subculture that further diminishes the magnitude of the disorder.

The consequences of compulsive buying can be devastating. Bankruptcy and divorce are frequent outcomes. But prior to these tragedies the individual suffers more subtly. Compulsive buyers have more bank credit cards and pay fewer of them off each month. They have over twice as much monthly debt and they often feel guilty and remorseful following shopping. As the debt increases, arguments over money also increase. Unserviceable debt leads to repossession of one's property and ultimately bankruptcy, while spouses give up on marriage in anger and frustration.

Appropriate psychological treatment is frequently the only way to break this cycle. This also includes abandoning buying as a solution to the pain in one's life. Instead of buying a new item of clothing to feel better, or worse yet, to punish the spouse for some transgression, the compulsive buyer must learn to nurture one's self emotionally and to deal with life's problems more directly. Enhancing one's self-esteem, becoming more assertive, developing social skills, building a network of friends, discovering meaningful and creative activities, and looking inward for spiritual direction are all part of the recovery process. Recovery requires experienced professional direction and access to therapeutic and self-help resources to provide the breadth of treatment necessary. If you are wondering if you are a compulsive buyer you probably are.

CASE STUDY #1: JEREMY

Jeremy was a trust fund kid, although he was no longer a kid. Now 35 years of age, he has never made a successful adjustment to adult life. He is of above average intelligence, owns his own home in a middle-class neighborhood, and is a physically attractive man. He does not have to work and has an annual income of around $75,000 from trust fund money he manages and from a monthly allotment administered by his family's trust. Jeremy can do a variety of things well. He is mechanically adept, is well versed in the stocks and bonds market, understands tax law, and is well-read. You may ask, How can anyone with all these advantages have a problem? Jeremy is also the product of severe physical and emotional abuse. He has no friends and he has not had an intimate relationship of any sort in ten years. Jeremy is a very unlikable person. He is critical and judgmental, and he is condescending and insensitive. He is also a compulsive buyer. Because of his financial security and acumen Jeremy will never suffer financially because of his compulsive buying. He has the wisdom to keep his income and investments secure but he cannot break the cycle of compulsive buying. Jeremy shops daily through the newspapers and magazines that sell used products. He is constantly running ads to buy and sell things. He rarely makes any money on these transactions and there is a never ending flow of goods into Jeremy's home.

Jeremy has ten electric toothbrushes, eight electric shavers, three refrigerators, over 160 guns, at least one of every electronic device known to man and in many cases three or four of each. There is barely room to walk through the rooms of his house and his yard is similarly filled with goods. He has about 40 tires of different sizes and wear, 12 bicycles, 5 boats, 8 outboard motors, 7 vehicles of different makes, 3 motorcycles, and a multitude of year-old tools.

At times, Jeremy has been in trouble with his neighbors because of the junk in his yard. When this occurs he goes through great turmoil cleaning up, organizing, donating goods to charitable organizations, and selling what he can. Once the crisis with the neighbors has passed, Jeremy goes back to his nonstop buying.

Jeremy states he would like to have friends but is afraid to have anyone over to his house because he realizes they will probably reject him once they see how he lives. To compensate for his social needs he continues to buy. His entire social life revolves around buying and selling in an often hostile manner.

Jeremy's compulsive buying is rooted in his childhood abuse. He has very low self-esteem, and feels a sense of worth and gratification in both buying and possessing things. He derives social status through having the financial resources to buy whatever he wants and frequently shows up at garage sales and swap meets with a big roll of cash. He enhances his status by bartering and haggling about prices and feels a sense of power and control when he walks away from a possible purchase. Jeremy has a rich fantasy world that borders on delusion; his possessiveness, envy, and total lack of generosity contribute greatly to his social isolation. Jeremy's circumstances are extreme but they highlight the extent to which compulsive buying can develop and impair one's ability to live a normal life.

CASE STUDY #2: RACHAEL

Rachael is a 38-year-old woman who is married to Bob, a civil engineer. Bob is employed by a large international construction company and also does part-time consulting. He works approximately sixty hours per week to "stay ahead of the bill collectors," as he puts it. Eight years ago the firm Bob worked for went out of business. He was out of work for about three months and during that time filed for personal bankruptcy. They had no savings, their home was mortgaged to the hilt, and they had approximately $60,000 in consumer debt. With the bills piling up, no savings, no equity, and no more borrowing power, they took the path of least resistance. If Bob lost his job today they would be facing another bankruptcy and probably a divorce. Rachael, you see, is a compulsive buyer. Her compulsive buying has been a source of conflict in her relationship with Bob for many years. Bob loves Rachael dearly but is tired of the instability her spending creates in their lives. He is tired of working long hours to support her spending and he is tired of their arguments.

Rachael is overweight by about fifty pounds. She is an only child. She has a horrible relationship with her mother. She has no relationship with her father and she has no extended family who care about her. Except for Bob and her children she is alone in the world. She has a very low opinion of herself and takes very few risks outside of spending too much.

Rachael shops daily. She shops for groceries, household items, clothes, cosmetics, items for her children, and gifts for everyone. Her daily shopping trips are the high point of her day. She knows the salespersons in the stores she shops in by their first names and they know hers. They tell her of upcoming sales and how to get the best bargains. She believes that with these relationships established she is a superior shopper. It is true that she gets great bargains, but it is also true that there is little room in their home for any more things. Rachael has three closets full of clothes. She also has clothes in her children's closets and in the garage. She also owns over a hundred pairs of shoes, a similar number of belts, jewelry, and accessories.

Rachael has a rich fantasy world filled with images of power, beauty, success, and, most of all, acceptance. She acknowledges her problem but she can scarcely go a day without shopping and always has a good reason why she must shop.

Rachael has fallen into a familiar cycle of feeling bad about herself and shopping to feel better. Shopping provides her with very positive social contacts (salespersons), it allows her to feel rich and powerful and to fulfill her fantasies. She feels a sense of deservedness from all her possessions and enjoys being surrounded by them.

However, her possessions also cause her guilt. She rarely wears or uses her purchases in part because she has so many and her buying pushes her husband Bob away, both by his avoidance of her and the resentment her problem causes him.

Rachael is in desperate need of treatment for her compulsive disorder. Without it the pattern will continue and in all likelihood, Bob will divorce her once the children are close to adulthood. Rachael needs to see a professional who has experience treating compulsive disorders. In a small percentage of cases (perhaps 30 percent) medication can assist. Psychologists familiar with compulsive disorders will assist in finding the origin of the problem and help the patient work through the pain of these most fundamental issues. Group therapy may also be suggested.

Regardless of the mode of treatment, it should be very clear that Rachael needs professional help. Without it her life will continue to deteriorate over time and her personal pain will only get worse.

Arlene Matthews, in her book on the psychology of money, told how Walter Cavanaugh of Santa Clara, California ended up in the *Guinness Book of World Records* for having over a thousand credit cards issued in his name, and an average of four arriving daily. Though Cavanaugh's wallet weighs 35 pounds and contains $1.5 million in buying power, he only has approximately 12 percent of all the cards available to the general public.

(Author's note: Dr. Booraem maintains his clinical practice in Santa Ana, CA.)

• • •

AUTHOR'S ANALYSIS

In business, borrowing is a necessary part of developing and maintaining a particular endeavor. When a company sells stock, it is in effect borrowing capital from prospective owners by offering a piece of the company. The money is then repaid in dividends and a greater value of ownership if the enterprise becomes more successful.

When a company needs equipment and cannot pay cash, it often finances what it needs with the expectation that the use of the equipment will generate enough revenue to eventually pay it off or at least make the monthly payment; at the same time, the company wants this equipment to help it grow. If the company deals with a number of suppliers, it is desirable to get "terms" from them where they can be paid at least thirty days after the goods or services are delivered rather than by COD. This allows the business to continue to use money that has already been spent.

Unless the company pays its employees daily, it is also "borrowing" their wages until it must distribute those funds on payday. It is common these days to see workers get paid once or twice a month, as opposed to the past norm of once a week.

Companies often find it necessary to secure lines of credit with banks in order to expand, get past slow periods, or develop to certain levels of production and profit. Government follows the same patterns. Professionals and social, religious, or educational organizations also accept and utilize borrowing at some level.

It seems clear that borrowing is part of the human condition. In addition to money, many other things can be borrowed—sugar, tools, clothes, water, vehicles, houses, even other people. Intangibles can be borrowed: time, sleep, an identity, an idea. If borrowing is a part of being human, and human beings have certain needs, it seems inevitable that a link between borrowing and those needs would exist in human societies.

Since in American society almost any need can be purchased with money, it is considered normal to do so. When is the borrowing of money considered "abnormal"? When the borrowing leads to some painful, undesirable result, or indirectly threatens that person or institution's existence within society.

Why, then, would anyone worry about the proliferation of credit cards? Because for the first time in human history, a little plastic, magnetically striped object can be used to satisfy every basic human need (food, water, shelter) and most, if not all, other needs as well.

Why should this cause concern? Because with a proliferation of credit cards comes the great proliferation of borrowing linked to needs.

If there are very few or no individuals who have all their needs met all the time, then there is a never ending market for credit cards. If borrowing, regardless of the fact that it is a "normal" behavior, was completely without negative consequences, then there would be no cause for concern. But we all know that there are many potential "bad" or abnormal things that can result from borrowing. As more people borrow to satisfy needs, the potential for negative results also increases.

I would submit that borrowing for food when one uses a credit card in the grocery store is the final link between the credit card and human needs. Thirty years ago the idea would have seemed abhorrent—only restaurant food, rather than day to day food, could be borrowed with a universal credit card. Credit card borrowing for the most basic needs has followed the great proliferation of credit cards themselves.

Mechanically, the *process* of linking credit cards to needs is obvious. No issuer runs an ad that reads, "Please use our card so that we can make big profits on your purchase while you are in debt for four or five years." Rather, the ad links a need of ours to the card itself: a happy couple walking hand in hand in some exotic country using a credit card; a distraught person in an airport getting a credit line increase so he can get home; a parent buying that special gift for his child using a credit card.

The stronger the emotion, the stronger the link. Our basic emotions are evoked and then used to link the card with the target need.

The tactic is as old as advertising itself. Products have always been pictured in the most positive light next to something obviously good or desirable. A new car is always shown shiny, clean, and fast. A new food is always shown with happy people at a nicely set table. The Old West medicine man was always well-dressed, standing on his soapbox, happy and healthy while reciting the great benefits of his Elixir of the Week.

How well would margarine sell if we only saw its true form—a drab, gray, manufactured substance rather than a smooth, buttery yellow spread? During World War II when butter was rationed and supplies of margarine were given out, food coloring was added to increase palatability.

After continued bombardment through advertising and media, do we accept the borrowing-for-needs link to our emotions because we are conditioned robots and leave it at that?

Of course not. We are beings with free will who often recognize the consequences of our actions. I do submit, however, that it is time to look at credit cards in a different way and create new strategies for the fact of their existence in today's society.

Alcohol and other drugs have existed within human societies from the beginning. Early on, *evaluations* were made that resulted in *regulation* of various substances. Some groups banned outright, while others emphasized moderation since they also recognized that the consequences of usage were not entirely negative. Is it not time to look at wide-scale institutionalized borrowing in the same way and come up with parameters for this type of activity?

Isn't unrestricted borrowing, especially on high-interest

credit cards, very similar to other vices like drugs which society already regulates? What is at stake?

From the issues raised in this book and the stories of people who sustained damage of some sort from "overindulgence," a reasonable person could conclude that the dangers are great and very real.

If the bankruptcy rate continues to rise, arguably so will the price of goods and services. With price increases can come a rise in inflation all the way down the line. What price is paid in American society as a whole when a large segment of the population continues to carry and service large amounts of debt? Isn't it burdensome enough to have a mortgage and one or two car payments without a new form of everyday debt that is taken for granted and accepted without question?

The thirty-year mortgage is a relatively new concept, having become the "norm" after the Depression years in the early part of the 20th century. The 4-5 year car loan is also a relatively new concept, becoming the "norm" since the 1970s. Now we already have two or three generations of Americans who carry semipermanent credit card debt every month as a "norm." Why not take steps now to say, "Hey, this should not be considered normal and healthy. We as a society recognize the potential for harm and the potential for abuse related to overspending/overborrowing. We will draw lines here and there to keep it in perspective and under control."

Do we not treat the most common drug, alcohol, in the same way? Once having banned it altogether in turn creating a criminal subclass that still exists today, we endeavored instead to regulate this drug.

Nowadays, "regulation" has become a dirty word and makes many people cringe. One reason is that there are too many regulations and rules in our society. The other reasons include the fact that many of the rules are ill-conceived and overdone, and then inefficiently monitored or implemented.

Many argue there is a permanently entrenched segment of society loosely labeled "bureaucrats" whose sole function is to create and enforce rules, thus propagating their own existence forever.

Many will argue that government on different levels is the main culprit; we hear every day "government can't do anything right." Nevertheless, if government help, rather than straight interference, is needed to enforce regulation, then it must be utilized.

We could design and implement reasonable regulations concerning the advertising of credit cards in various media outlets, especially television. Why was a ban on hard liquor in television ads imposed? Because society drew a line between wine and beer and "hard" liquor. This is the same type of reasoning that led to the enactment of drinking-age laws in many states that delineate different legal ages for the purchase or consumption of different kinds of alcohol; specifically beverages with different *amounts* of alcohol in them.

Now, with blatant, daily pitches on television aimed at citizens with all the manipulative skill Madison Avenue can muster, it is time to draw the line again. When credit card grantors aim their wares specifically at the very young, as evidenced by college campus and high school sign-up campaigns, responsible citizens are obligated to create a set of circumstances when it is not only "normal" but imperative for the ad target to *Just say no*.

There are many schools that teach mathematics. There are many schools that teach business, which is applied mathematics, among other things. There are many schools that teach personal finance. But how many schools universally teach that too much debt is to be avoided at all costs? Certainly the evils of debt are discussed at some point in every high school or junior high curriculum, but where is it taught or preached on the same level and at the same volume that "Just

Say No To Drugs" is? Almost every school kid has heard and continues to hear this phrase since the '80s. It's time to coin a new phrase, something like, "Just say no to overspending and permanent consumer debt."

Under a continual onslaught by credit grantors of "spend, spend, spend," it is not enough to mumble, "more education is needed."

Responsible citizens can adopt the methods of the advertising pros. The borrowing/need emotional link should be counterbalanced with a consequence-based link. Hasn't this worked very well with cigarette smoking?

Cigarette smoking was once considered "cool," "glamorous," and associated with good health. Now what reasonable person would advocate those so-called benefits on behalf of smoking? Tobacco use was pegged as an unhealthy, addictive behavior and regulations were promulgated which treat it as such. The result is that less people smoke and the population is more healthy.

Ads on MTV make fun of smoking and point out its bad effects. This is done to show young and inexperienced people data that counterbalances the positive-linked messages they receive about smoking from other sources like already hooked parents and peers. We must do the same with credit cards and *overspending as a way of life*.

Concurrently with proper teaching in the schools, we must have proper teaching in the home. This is a tough one. How many parents use credit cards daily in front of their children as opposed to those who smoke cigarettes or drink in front of their kids? How many children witness their parents use credit cards at the grocery store, convenience store, or fast food joint? Of those who do, how many see any of the effects on their family's short- and long-term finances—the effect on what is actually spent on credit-obtained goods, what is left for other goods, what is left for savings and investment? What kind of, if any, explanations are offered to children by parents who continually use credit in their presence? How many parents even recognize this as an issue and ever consider whether an explanation should be offered or what kind of example they are setting?

As an eternal optimist, I believe that while we become temporarily blind or indifferent to certain issues, Americans in general are a savvy, independent-minded lot.

The history of America is one of saying *no* to manipulation and control from assorted monarchs, demagogues, and institutions. When threatened from within or without, the typical American has always reached for his or her weapons.

Why, then, have large segments of our populace chosen to crown the credit grantor king, and given an almost religious status to the credit card? Part of the answer may lie in our history of struggle with poverty and the fact that we have one of the largest middle classes in world history.

When Europeans began colonizing and building America, they were more often than not poor or disenfranchised members of the society they came from. Upon arrival here, they were required to work hard or perish. This chiefly agricultural society was composed of self-contained units: families or small communities which grew most of what was needed for survival. Excess crops were bartered for goods that were needed but not locally produced.

Established, European-based trading companies backed by monarchy-controlled "money houses" (banks) brought goods in and out of the small communities.

After the advent of the Industrial Revolution and struggles like the Civil War and unionization, society was forever changed. With mass production of goods came mass proliferation of goods—they had to be distributed. Distribution then became more dependent on *selling by persuasion* as the number of different goods exceeded those that were strict necessities.

For example, after one has food, shelter, and clothing, one has everything that is necessary for bare survival. One can then argue that any material good acquired beyond those things is superfluous; mere icing on the cake where minimum survival is concerned.

But the factories of the Industrial Revolution were turning out thousands of different products that were not necessary to bare survival. These goods had to be sold or the industries would perish, so a whole new subclass of society came to prominence—the institutionalization of persuasion in the persona of the "salesman." No longer mere horse traders, salesmen became the knights of industry, the force entrusted with the mission of proliferation.

Peasants are those who own little or nothing and just barely survive. Rulers or the ruling class have everything that they desire. At this juncture in American history (early 20th century; pre WW II) more Americans had more goods than ever before. Though some stayed "peasants," and some became members of the "ruling class," most were now part of the growing "middle class."

This class stopped growing and fell on its face when the Great Depression hit. Again, there was mainly "rich" and "poor." World War II changed everything and the 1950s saw the middle class once again rise and achieve an economic level never before attained. Many of those who had lived through the Depression, World War II, and this subsequent rebirth, vowed that they would never be poor again. For many, "poor" is equated with not having enough material goods. So, perhaps we can mark the 1950s as the period when materialism as a way of life started to become the norm for many Americans.

Is it a coincidence, then, that the 1950s also saw the birth of credit cards as we know them today?

What I find most interesting is the great disparity between the generations from the early 20th century and those born later, in their respective approaches to money and debt.

Specifically, I almost always see a great difference in attitude concerning money and credit between a person born before the late 1940s and a person born after those years—a baby boomer vs. non-baby boomer categorization.

Assuming that I am dealing with an individual who is, by definition, "middle class," the characteristics I have observed in my practice are as follows:

The non-baby boomer uses credit routinely for larger purchases like a car or major appliance. He or she carries credit cards but generally views them as something to use as backup or in an emergency. They are more likely to use an American Express card for business and pay the charges in full each month instead of using a revolving Visa or MasterCard.

The non-baby boomer also has some sort of savings, if not in a designated bank account or retirement plan, then at least in a home with substantial equity he considers his nest egg.

This individual views nonmajor, everyday debt with suspicion, and will often verbalize it as "bad." If he ends up in bankruptcy or other financial trouble, it is more often than not a result of a "catastrophe" like divorce, underinsured illness, job loss, etc. During the bankruptcy process they will communicate shame and a sense of failure for having had to file. In his mind there is a *stigma* attached to bankruptcy or financial failure.

The non-baby boomer has acquired many material goods throughout life, but these were acquired *slowly* over extended periods of time. They often possess a few "toys" like a boat or a motorcycle, but these items are usually balanced out by a large number of practical items like furniture.

The baby boomer will not necessarily be entirely opposite with respect to the above-mentioned observations. The differences are often subtle and not readily apparent:

The baby boomer tends to use credit almost daily, wants to pay the bill at the end of the month, but often ends up leaving a small balance as revolving debt. He has some savings, but doesn't have a *plan* for doing so; more discretionary income seems to be spent instead of saved. He seems to possess more luxury goods in proportion to practical goods than his older counterparts. He likes to acquire goods *now* rather than later. When financial disaster strikes it is more often than not due to too liberal use of lines of credit. A big difference I see is in their attitude toward bankruptcy. While they still project shame and failure, there is much less acknowledgment that they have acquired any kind of stigma. This is not surprising, since I have had many clients who received new credit card solicitations before their bankruptcy case had even ended!

There is an ongoing controversy about whether baby boomers are economically better off than their parents.

In September of 1993, the Congressional Budget Office released a report which claimed that the 76 million Americans born between 1946 and 1964 are "financially better off than their parents' generation was as young adults," with the exception of those who had dropped out of high school. The study was based on census data and consumer surveys.

With adjustment made for differences in the dollar's buying power and value, the study found the median income of baby boomers to be $38,400 in 1989. By comparison, people the same age in 1959 had a median income of $25,100. The study also came up with $47,000 as the 1989 median income for families where the wife worked, at the same time acknowledging that the dollar value of mothers who stayed at home was not measured.

I find this largely irrelevant and worthless in terms of

describing what is really happening. Admittedly, I harbor certain built-in prejudices which skew my observations and opinions: whenever the "government" says something I automatically disbelieve the statement because unlike most scientific researchers, various parts of the government, whether they be representative or bureaucratic in nature, have a vested interest in their own perpetuation and are filled with political appointees and those who acquired positions through nepotism.

Like business, which exists to make a profit, government has its own agenda that often competes with pure scientific inquiry; facts are presented by "spin doctors" who propagandize in order to meet the entity's particular needs.

The "profit" or efficiency of a governmental entity is supposed to be measured in terms of how well it meets the needs of its citizenry, its purported employer. So I am just as suspicious of a government-generated "study" that tells me "things are better than ever before" as I am when a company I own stock in tells me the same thing. The message in both cases stems from an interested party—one which can advance its own position by slanting the facts. Therefore, I think for myself and test any information which opposes what I know or believe. Since I don't know or believe baby boomers to have a better lifestyle, I tend to disbelieve the communications which state otherwise.

If more wives work outside the home, then gross income should be higher, and apparently is. But, if more money is spent for taxes and material goods that depreciate in value, what is the *net* asset gain over 20-30 years? In other words, what position will such a couple be in financially when they are ready to retire as compared to the generations before? Isn't that the real test if we are measuring who was "better off"? Or is "better off" measured by how much the people were able to *consume* during their working lives?

While it can be argued that greater consumption brings greater satisfaction, hence greater "happiness," at what point are certain other costs made part of the equation?

Many people believe that the emotional cost to the family of a working mother is too high. There have been scores of studies, books, programs, etc. that continue to explore and debate the effect of a working mother on children. Many have concluded that there is no "right" answer because of the many variables involved.

If one accepts this as true, then the concept of "better off" becomes meaningless and irrelevant and therefore so does the aforementioned study.

Perhaps we can say that the acquisition of material goods is a measure of success for most members of a thriving middle class. If so, then we could also say that the *manner* and *type* of goods acquired will vary according to age and values. "Whoever dies with the most toys wins" is not a rallying cry for all of middle-class America.

I've spoken to many people over the age of sixty who lived during decades where most women did not work outside the home. The question I always ask is, "Do you think people are better off economically nowadays with two paychecks than thirty years ago when only one paycheck was coming in?"

While this type of informal survey is hardly scientific in nature, I always seem to get similar answers.

The great majority seem to feel that the number of luxury, nonnecessity goods in the typical home is much greater now than thirty years ago.

More than one television, multiple electronic entertainment modules, two or more cars, are often mentioned. The answers usually include lists of things common in the home today which were acquired early without waiting 10-15 years to accumulate them.

There are many more single or divorced people over age

thirty now than in the 1960s. These individuals also seem to own more goods than in the past. This is a difficult comparison, though, because this subclass did not exist in its present form in the 1960s.

Everyone, it seems, brings up the issue of "quality of life;" those intangibles like "happiness," "greater self-worth," and "day-to-day enjoyment." Much has been written about the great stresses of modern life on individuals and both "traditional" and "nontraditional" families with the majority opinion being that stress has greatly increased in the last 20 to 30 years.

Therefore, the question must be asked, "If we have all this great 'stuff,' shouldn't we be happier"? When credit card issuers push us to spend more and acquire more things, aren't they just trying to give us what we need more of?

Those with strong religious and/or philosophical beliefs may answer that the above issues are explained by a present decline in "spiritual" or "humanistic" values. They point to the age-old truths that say the "material world" is not all there is to life, or even its true essence.

Every day, politicians get positive responses when they proclaim that we must return to "traditional values," that modern life has abandoned certain ancient maxims, and that most, if not all, present-day problems can be solved by returning to "tradition."

Even when my least favorite politician makes such a statement, I must recognize that it contains much truth. Traditions have evolved in human cultures over thousands of years for very good reasons, most of which are related to the survival and perpetuation of our species. Just as we evolved biologically from simpler animals, our species has developed behavior patterns which help insure "survival of the fittest." (Yes, my Fundamentalist Friends, I believe in evolution. Been to a museum, zoo, or library lately?) So, again, is the drive to consume related to survival? Food gathering exists as a fundamental behavior of all living things. Obviously no living thing would survive without food, and each has some process from mere chemical reactions to complex behaviors to feed itself.

In present-day America, rampant consumerism might just be a complex extension of food gathering; we gather not only food, but numerous material goods that our brains somehow have linked to the same "survive and prosper program" that drives us to gather food. Is it a coincidence that supermarkets routinely carry many different kinds of goods other than food? The existence of a supermarket is a relatively new concept in human society, such stores having evolved from smaller ones.

Is it surprising, then, to see huge warehouse-type stores become popular and thrive when they carry every consumer good imaginable in addition to vast quantities of food in bulk?

If there is a true evolutionary process at work here, where is it leading? Should we expect larger and larger warehouses of consumer goods, perhaps taking up several blocks each, requiring people to be transported within them like an amusement park? Would such structures take on a sacred quality as "temples of survival" linked to the already ingrained drive to consume? Even now, such stores contain everything a human being needs to live. A recent movie showed a young couple "living" within a department store for one night. While doing so they engaged in every form of human behavior, all without leaving the store.

Perhaps this process is leading to future self-contained cities sealed off from the rest of the world, similar to ancient walled cities. The great difference would be that such cities would be truly self-contained, needing no food, air, or water from the outside world.

A recent experiment in Arizona showed that this is possible now. A group of scientists actually lived in a sealed-off habitat for many months. While certain systems went awry, the experiment showed that sealed environments for human beings have become present reality.

In order to find real solutions to overspending or credit problems, fact finding must go to a deeper level than it ever has before. If one believes that overspending on credit is linked to survival drives, is it enough to educate ourselves and our children only on things like balancing a checkbook, avoiding frivolous debt, and preserving capital for the future? Even if such "solutions" could be implemented quickly and every citizen had this knowledge, would problems necessarily disappear?

Any answer may lie in the alcoholism analogy. If one accepts the view that alcoholism is a disease and that all diseases have a chemical-molecular foundation, then it follows that any "treatment" must address this fact. Today, research into alcoholism suggests a genetic basis, perhaps even a specific gene that when "switched on" gives a person a disposition and tendency to become an alcoholic. Should we be looking for a "compulsiveness gene" that might make some people have a tendency to overspend, i.e. squander survival-necessary resources even when armed with all necessary logic and education on such matters?

Or should we follow the Alcoholics Anonymous approach in dealing with what can be called a "compulsion disease"? AA uses a 12-step program to arrest the disease. They make it clear that there is no "cure"—the individual is now and always will be an alcoholic. If the process is successful, the person will not *consume* and can be said to be "recovering," but they are never cured.

Summarizing issues from questions posed above, we have inquiries that look like this:

What causes individuals to overspend? If overspending

is bad, what can be done to stop it? When overspending is done on credit, rather than funds on hand, what does this mean for the individual and society?

Addressing these questions, I start with the premise that rampant consumerism is related to survival. So, if you accept my opinion that this is a "problem," it follows that solutions will be based on breaking the connection between overconsuming and surviving.

If you accept my second premise that overspending on credit is even worse, then I believe that it also follows that the solutions to this problem should be more intensive than solutions to the first.

As shown earlier in this volume, when the subject of consumer knowledge comes up, almost everyone says, "More education is needed." Great, but what kind of education?

First I believe that we must recognize consumption as a behavior and teach it as such, starting in elementary school. Sound strange? Well, it's really not. Don't we now have elementary school instruction in "accepted" behaviors like personal hygiene, manners, social etiquette, etc.? Don't we already teach behaviors like how to treat others, how to act (or not act) in a group, and the difference between right and wrong?

Do we not teach children that they are supposed to learn specific things to prepare them for adult life? Do we not expose them to knowledge in order to help them follow their talents and tendencies in order to become "productive members of society"? And do we not give them negative reinforcement (punishment) when they do not follow the "acceptable" patterns?

I propose that it is high time to come up with a set of facts regarding consumerism that a majority of Americans can agree upon, and start *teaching* them, in the schools and in the home. Such facts would include:

"You will need a certain number of things in life to do what you wish to within this society, these include…"

"In order to acquire these things you will need to generate income."

"The acceptable methods of generating income in our society are…"

"If you intend to live within society (as opposed to outside of it or as a member of its underclass), here is how it works: [Basic economic structure—what happens to money after it is earned, what a standard of living is, what income is needed to achieve various standards of living, how to earn money, how to manage money, and what happens when money is mismanaged]."

Certainly these concepts are widely taught now, but I submit that they are being taught in a haphazard and disorganized manner.

We should teach, again in a standardized format that all future citizens can understand, why people act or do not act in certain ways—i.e. why smart people do stupid things, what a societal subculture is and what behaviors characterize it, what behaviors are particularly destructive to *individuals*, *families*, and *society*, and *why* we categorize such behaviors as "destructive."

As described earlier, most citizens are taught, "say no to drugs," but how many are simultaneously given all the "ways" and reasons to "say no"? Isn't it indisputable that the young, particularly young Americans, need more than a simple "don't" in order to nurture true positive behavior? Has anyone met an adolescent, for example, that never questioned authority? Isn't it time to go beyond sloganism and oversimplicity and come up with a well-thought out, rational approach to dealing with these issues?

If yes, then we should add overspending and overspending on credit to the list of destructive behaviors. The evidence supporting such a distinction is overwhelming—personal and business bankruptcies are filed in great numbers, governments routinely carry huge deficits, the nationwide divorce rate is high, more mothers work outside the home than ever before, more new high school and college graduates can't find the job they want or were trained for, less prospective businesspeople or entrepreneurs can find a field they can make a profit in, or the capital to enter it, and personal debt is at its highest level ever.

Once a standardized educational format is agreed upon and implemented, we must continue to identify the causes that lead to destructive spending behavior and come up with strategies to either neutralize or eradicate them. This will be the hardest part. Why? Because I think we will then have come up against the same groups which stymie progress in other areas—vested, well-financed, powerful special interests.

These might include: banks which make or attempt to make great profits on the debt of others; their cousins like thrifts, savings and loans, and finance companies; corporations which need to produce huge quantities of consumer goods; merchants/retailers which sell these goods to consumers on credit; the individuals who run and own these entities—officers and other employees, stockholders, etc.; media organs which make great profits on the promulgation of debt and consuming on credit—television, radio, newspapers; the resort industry, particularly those which rely on gambling; certain governmental entities which exist because of destructive spending (take your pick).

Hopefully, at this point there will be enough citizenry and other interest groups to counterbalance those who might not want to see a reduction in consumer debt. Such groups might include existing ones like Common Cause, certain insurance companies which might write more policies, and therefore collect more premiums if less money was spent servicing consumer debt; smaller credit unions which might make more profits if savings are increased and less debt is incurred with larger institutions; savings and loans and other mortgage lenders which might be able to make better profits on mortgages if less money is used for other types of debt; also, educational institutions and religious groups for similar reasons. If it could weather the predictable political storm, what would this "reform process" be focusing on?

Identifying destructive credit behaviors that exist despite our knowledge of their causes. This would conceivably take place during the same time frame that the education reforms are being implemented, and our attempted identification of the actual causes of such behavior is going on. In a practical sense, it would probably be better to think of this process as something other than a "straight line," as different parts of it would develop at different rates in different geographical parts of the country.

Who would lead this movement to identify and solve current credit abuse problems?

The logical answer would seem to be leaders from the counterbalance groups listed above. These groups already contain structures which are suitable for goal-setting and implementation because of their very nature as organizations. Therefore I believe that this would not be nor should be what is commonly known as a "grass roots movement." Not that I have anything against such endeavors—I recognize that the history and origin of this country is full of positive results that came about because of spontaneous, grass roots efforts.

Rather, I believe that the problems at hand require fast, formally structured, well-financed, *organizational* solving efforts in order to counterbalance what I see as the forces which will be opposed to eradication or neutralization.

Should we look to governmental leaders (i.e. politicians) to spearhead this effort? I believe not. It is my further belief that they do their best work when pressured from without, by citizens within strong groups.

So, while my model "credit reform entity" must necessarily include government-employed individuals and governmental agencies, I would not start with them.

Leaders of the aforementioned counter groups should form an organization to identify problems like those I've touched upon, and develop strategies to solve them. As the benefits become known, individual people will naturally support and become part of this organization and policy makers will then have to take heed.

Ironically, this organization would need to be driven by some type of profit motive, rather than intangible, esoteric aspirations. Why? Because this has been shown to be the strongest in accomplishing economic goals within human societies. Examples such as capitalism vs. socialism abound. If one defines "profit" as the net gain after "overhead" from one's efforts, then everything we do involves some desire for profit. Even when we give away money or an object, expecting "nothing" in return, are we not doing so in expectation of an emotional/spiritual benefit; a gain or something more than what we already had?

This work has touched upon and described in anecdotal form many problems associated with credit, especially bank cards. It also advocates my ideas about organizing an entity to attempt to solve these problems. Now seems like a good time to attempt to more formally list these issues in order to give future reformers a good starting point. Also, readers, assumed to be concerned citizens, can use this as a beginning for their own inquiries.

Why Do Credit Card Issuers Focus on the Very Young?

I define "very young" as the 18-24-year-old age group. Since I am not privy to the marketing strategies currently in use by various issuers, I do not know the extent of such focus. I do know, however, from firsthand observation and input from peers, that: credit card issuers send applications to high school seniors; credit card issuers set up tables with applications on college campuses; credit card issuers run ads on youth-oriented television programs, to name a few examples of marketing aimed at the very young. Basic marketing says that a customer gained early and kept satisfied can become a customer for life. This is a great benefit to the issuer.

Basic mathematics helps shed light: If a $1,000 loan (i.e. balance on a credit card) is incurred at age twenty-four, at say 18 percent interest and is paid off by minimum monthly payments of $35, repayment would then be completed near age twenty-seven, a significant amount of time in a person's life. This is a period of time most businesses would *love* to have a person as a customer. Plus, the longer the relationship, the greater the chance that the person will remain a customer.

When an established credit card customer is extended *more* credit, then they are more likely to use it, especially if the previous limit has been reached.

Almost all would agree that money habits, like most other habits, are established early in life. So, if a young person gets in the habit of using credit cards early, it can be concluded that they will continue to use cards throughout their lives, a great benefit to issuers in general, and the particular issuer who first made them a customer.

As credit cards became *required* for certain things such as renting a car, hotel room, or ordering something by phone, the person has to carry one or risk becoming a member of society's underclass.

Do not most parents use *conditioning* (reward or punishment for various actions until the child gets it right) on babies to change their behavior to "acceptable" modes?

Isn't credit card issuance to the very young just another

form of conditioning?

Why Are Credit Cards Now Required For So Many Transactions?

As economist Kamin mentions above, banks, retailers, government, and others "love" credit cards for a variety of good reasons. Convenience and profit are, as in most other human endeavors, the two great general reasons.

While I can hardly deny these motivations or say they are meaningless, I can and do say that it's time to put our foot down and demand a different system. The questions we must ask are endemic to issues of personal freedom:

Do we want to create a permanent record of our financial transactions for various entities, both in business and in government to see? (Does anyone believe that our transaction records are or will ever be hidden from the wrong eyes?) Do we want our *freedom of movement* to be dependent on what a credit card issuer determines to be our "creditworthiness" (ability to rent a car, hotel room, apartment, purchase plane tickets by phone)?

Already there are those advocating that a complete credit report should no longer be used for renting an apartment—just a credit card in good standing. So if this comes to pass, your refusal or inability to pay a certain credit card issuer's bill can mean you cannot rent in your own town.

What about gas stations that are going electronic? Is it farfetched to see a time when you will always need a credit card to buy gas?

Another interesting phenomenon along the same lines that I've observed in my practice is the cancellation of credit cards where the person has filed for bankruptcy. No, I'm not referring to accounts with balances listed in the bankruptcy petition—I'm talking about clear, unused, zero balance cards which are not listed in the case because no debt existed at the time of filing. The issuer finds out about the bankruptcy through a credit bureau and then cancels the person's account, even though that issuer *sustained no loss.*

At first you may say, so what, bankrupt people shouldn't have credit cards. But looking a bit deeper, what has occurred? One issuer/credit source has penalized the consumer for a loss that a separate, distinct creditor has suffered from that person.

This in and of itself is not too unusual—years ago, if you didn't pay your local grocer, wouldn't the butcher find out and temporarily cut off your credit? But here, the grantor is completely severing the relationship with you on the basis of a third party's report, based on an act it only knows occurred, not caring about the reasons *why* it occurred. (Maybe someone in your family contracted a disease requiring six-figure treatment, there was not enough insurance, and a personal bankruptcy became necessary).

Further, you have been severed from a relationship that is fast becoming a necessity for modern life.

Why Are Multiple Credit Cards Issued So Freely?

Almost all the consumer bankruptcy cases I've handled involved the person having more than one of a certain type of bankcard, such as a MasterCard or Visa, each with its own account number and credit line.

Many of my clients had several Visa or MasterCard accounts with the same bank, as do my wife and I, and most people we know.

The reason for this is obvious—the more cards that are issued, the greater the potential for profit. Supposedly, accounts are opened and cards are issued according to "creditworthiness," a concept that has taken on different meanings for different situations.

The "credit scoring system" is still in wide use in this country. This is where certain "positive" traits like a bank account, home ownership, or a certain income/debt ratio are assigned a number of points. If enough points are earned, then the credit is granted.

Another way cards are issued is by "preferred lists." The prospective customer's various traits are matched to an issuer's profile for those it wants to solicit. The person gets an invitation or "preapproved" certificate in the mail to sign up and receive an account. Many times clients of mine, still in the middle of their bankruptcy, have received such solicitations in the mail.

Should one individual or couple be issued an unlimited number of one type of bank card? Is such promulgation an open invitation to overspend? What true benefits are there to a customer if they carry multiple cards?

It seems to me that the potential for trouble far outweighs any benefits. First, regardless of what may be issued, everyone has a true credit limit which is never determined by any third party—no existing evaluation or scoring system takes all spending or income of a person into account—they are all just *models*, which can only mimic real life.

If this is correct, then it must follow that only the individual can determine what his limit should be. How much unsecured credit is adequate? Ideally, it is that which can be comfortably paid in full thirty days later when the bill arrives, rather than in installments over many months.

How often do we put full payment off for a month in order to use those funds for one thing or another? When done on a widespread scale, how many millions of dollars *per day* are generated by finance charges?

I have encountered many people who financed a business start-up or similar project on credit cards. Of course, most of the individuals I've encountered *failed* using this method. Why? Because the interest rates are so high. If one is starting a business expected to yield a small amount of profit, especially in the first few years, finance charges in the high teens, due monthly with principal payments, can quickly send the enterprise down the tubes.

Another thing I've seen many times is the "things will get better soon" syndrome—the person convinces himself against what he already knows—that it is now okay to borrow thousands of dollars on plastic because "my tax refund will be $3,000 and I can payoff the account," "I'll be getting a big Christmas bonus," "I'll certainly earn a commission large enough to pay this off in a couple of months." The present desire to have or do something *now* overwhelms common sense and a rationalization is created. It seems that more often than not, something else occurs or the expectation is never realized; but the bill must still be paid.

A particularly sad situation is where a medical emergency—often life-threatening—occurs and insurance is either non-existent or inadequate. The party uses bankcards, now accepted by most health-care providers, to get treatment or medicine.

What parent would hesitate to use their existing lines of credit if their child's life was on the line? At this point, what level of rationality can there be? Or, hasn't the consequence of financial ruin ceased to be relevant?

If credit card issuers are so willing to give out multiple cards, why are we willing to accept them without question? Most people like "getting things"—we give gifts or material goods to another to show love, respect, or thanks. Whatever happened to the old saying, "You don't get something for nothing"? Isn't this especially true for credit cards which have annual fees of $25 or more and high interest rates?

If more people refused to accept these "preapproved" cards, wouldn't issuers be forced to become more competitive? Would the day come where they might offer true benefits instead of sundry things like $2,000 life insurance or towing reimbursement? Has this already happened, thus the reason we see more rebate cards?

If there truly is a trend for more rebate/bonuses when credit cards are used, does this solve the overspending problem? No, it only perpetuates it. If the price of an item purchased on credit is made 20 percent higher because of finance charges, what's the big deal when you get a 1 percent rebate? Isn't this just another scheme to make us use the cards more and get ourselves permanently into debt?

The best "rebate" comes when you shop for an item, make your best deal, and pay cash. This is something most of us already know intellectually, but the "emotion invokers" are doing their best to make us "forget."

Why Do Banks "Love" Electronic Money?

As economist Kamin pointed out earlier, certain groups "love" credit cards, banks included. He neatly lays out some reasons why this is so. Additionally, we are faced with the growing prospect of pure electronic money, to the point where we will never handle bills or coin. The technology for this has existed for a long time. Why is it not present reality?

There are many reasons. First and foremost I believe is the public's distrust of the intangible, especially when it concerns something as survival-necessary as money. Many older people like my grandfather completely distrusted banks, regardless of government-sponsored insurance. For many years he kept his life savings in a hole he made in the basement floor, preferring to lose value to inflation rather than taking the risk of losing it all to a bank failure or governmental breakdown. Of course, this was a man who had fled Russia just before Lenin and his cronies took over, came to this country, worked hard, and became "middle class," only to suffer through the Great Depression. But people throughout recorded history have always hoarded tangible items like food, precious stones, gold, etc. in place of entrusting all their resources to others.

Again, the concept of banking as it exists today is brand new when viewed as an element of "civilized behavior." Now we have millions of working people who never get a paper paycheck—the funds are deposited electronically. Millions of Social Security recipients do the same thing. When this occurs, a pile of paper bills becomes an electronic blip, subject to someone else's control.

If this is so prevalent, why then do the great majority of American consumers still use paper checks? The reason is probably due to the "float" that checks give, even if only for one or two days. Years ago I knew a guy who had three checking accounts—one in California, one in Georgia, and one in New York. He claimed that for years he kept a check-kiting float going between the three banks—perpetually depositing checks from one account to cover checks he had written from another, rarely putting "new" money into his "system," thus getting free use of bank money. He said he was able to do this because a check from California would take more than a week to clear at one of the eastern banks.

Sometime in the late '70s his scheme collapsed, when electronic advances caused these checks to clear in just three or four days. Now, checks clear even faster. But a float still exists. This is because the paper still has to pass through human clerical hands before the great machines can process it.

Banks have been pushing "debit" cards for years, but most people don't use them. But most Americans use credit cards. It would appear that when it comes to funds on hand, the public likes to spend it by cash or check, but likes to augment or stretch it through the use of credit cards. This supposedly gives us more direct control of our liquid resources.

As credit cards become *required* for more purchases or transactions, the banks will probably get their way. It is less expensive to process blips than paper; blips are instantaneous while paper has to travel. In a world economy where our economic fate/future is quickly affected by what happened a couple of hours ago on the other side of the world, like it or not such a system is mandatory.

My clients often complain that when they first started getting into financial trouble and called their plastic creditors to try and make arrangements like lowered or suspended payments, most were cold or uncaring about their particular problem, even if it was something terrible like a major illness. They are shocked that they have been treated this way, such treatment literally pushing them to my door.

I remind the client of the great changes which have occurred in consumer lending in the last thirty years. In the past if an average consumer wanted a loan, they had to go in person and meet with the banker. After asking scores of questions, the banker would make a decision, often taking the applicant's attitude and personality into account as part of the granting process. If the borrower ran into trouble later during repayment, he could go and usually talk in person to the very same individual who approved the loan in the first place. Most of the time something could be worked out to get past the problem period.

Now, few borrowers ever meet their creditor's representative. Preapproved applications come in the mail, payments are sent to a post office box out of state, funds are disbursed in almost every bank just by the universal card's particular logo. This kind of impersonal interaction between consumer and creditor may work well until something happens. Then the person is forced to deal with a faceless customer service representative on the other end of an 800 number who knows little about them except for what the computerized account history may show.

This is a far cry from the local banker whose children may have been in the same class at school with those of the customer. Is it any wonder that the results then become so mechanical?

Today many of my clients will say something like, "I really hate doing this to [bankrupting on] my dentist, but Bank X can jump in the lake, they could care less about me, I'm just a speck in the computer."

At this point, I'll remind them that the impersonal, fast and easy way they obtained the credit in the first place has come full circle and worked against them—when trouble hit the creditor's reaction was just as fast and abrupt—"pay up or else—I don't want to hear about your personal problems."

Another reason for the continued existence of tangible money is the vast underground economy in this country and the rest of the world.

When Prohibition went into effect, we all know what happened: criminal elements quickly moved in and supplied the booze everyone demanded. Millions upon millions of dollars flowed directly into the hands of the criminal subclass. Not only did these huge amounts of money create rich gangsters, but the very same dollars served to finance many other types of criminal activity. Vast, well-financed organizations flourished and penetrated all parts of the national economy. Though I am not aware of any investment studies on this subject it would be fair to assume that growth from early 20th century Prohibition capital has made these enterprises what they are today.

Of course, none of this money went directly into state or federal treasuries, and the majority of these transactions were in cash.

Now we have a similar situation with drugs. Marijuana is the chief cash crop of several states. Cocaine, though imported, accounts for many billions of dollars in *cash*flow, U.S. sales in dollars being greater than the GNP of many nations.

The great difference between illicit cash flow today and in the 1930s is the greater sophistication of money laundering.

Unlike their predecessors, today's black marketeers make greater use of the regular banking system to move dollars. This has an enormous impact on the national and world economy. Vast amounts of paper bills remain necessary to keep these enterprises going.

In addition to illegal drugs, cash is required in many other black markets in the underground economy: gambling, prostitution, stolen merchandise, loan sharking.

Add to this what I call the "gray market"—sales and services which are performed strictly on a cash basis and not reported on income tax returns. Also, millions of illegal aliens work "off the books" for cash. This money is then spent on things like rent and food, finding its way back into the "regular" economy but without a piece going to Uncle Sam.

As long as these economic structures exist, cash will be necessary. It is undeniable that many transactions in the underground economy take place through the use of universal credit cards. Drug dealers routinely make sales on bank cards using legitimate business entities as a front, as do other criminals.

It therefore appears that a conflict is in progress regarding the billions of dollars flowing through the underground economy. On one hand you have the government, always in the red through deficit spending, needing enormous amounts of tax money each day to feed its voracious appetite. So it is a goal of many of the entities we label "government" to shut down certain enterprises to bring dollars through the "tax filter," so said entities can get their piece.

On the other hand, you have the "entrepreneurs" themselves who want to keep their activities hidden from governmental entities who not only keep tax dollars, but also control law enforcement, the police powers that shut illicit operations down.

In the middle you have banks and their progeny, universal

credit cards. Certainly there exists some sort of statistics or estimations of how many dollars or transactions due to the underground economy flow through universal credit cards. The impact has to be significant, since we already know that this structure is in the multibillions.

What is the true policy of these middlemen? Do they wish the flow to continue as is, quietly turning their heads? Have they calculated that *more* profits would be earned if cash was largely eliminated and all dollars were electronically accounted for and taxed? Are they neutral, perhaps having concluded that the results are unimportant? Or are they just not tuned in to this issue and truly ignorant of its effects?

Why don't you ask them?

Regulations Needed

Other than education in the home and schools, there are many things society can do collectively to keep credit card abuse and overspending under control. When we make laws, regulations, and policies, we act as a group for the common good. If such rules are logical, necessary, and carried out in a lawful, proper manner, then positive results occur.

Multiple credit cards are often abused. They exist in such great numbers because multiple issuers are anxious to get them into the hands of more and more consumers. It is in our best interests to put limits on this. While universal card accounts have their own dollar limits, the concept of a credit limit today has become largely meaningless.

It is not unusual, and is in fact common, to see minimum-wage earners with 5-10 thousand dollar universal gold cards in multiples. I can't recall how many times I have met with a very young person working on a first job, making perhaps $6 per hour, holding several universal cards with limits over $5,000. This is not "economic freedom," but an invitation to disaster. Continued greed by issuers has created situations where the individual can all too easily financially self-destruct.

Some may argue that the issuers will "police" this situation themselves, in order to avoid losses, something which is in their self-interest. I do not believe this to be true because the accounts are at such high interest rates while the actual cost of money remains low. It is clear that a default/loss rate is already built in; the enormous profits made on those who will make monthly payments "forever" will more than make up for those who disappear or file bankruptcy.

On the other hand, I do not advocate any sort of "ban" on holding multiple universal cards. Banning things often only creates greater demand for that which is forbidden, and is not a behavior or policy that endears most Americans to a desirable goal. Banning something, especially when done by government, comes with the implication that the beneficiary thereof is not smart, sophisticated, or knowledgeable enough to stay away from what is "bad" for them. While acceptable and necessary for children, this does not go over well with adults.

Rather than penalize people, regulations should reward them. What sort of rewards should be offered to citizens who voluntarily keep their multiple universal cards under a certain number (like 3 or less)?

First, we could reinstate the credit card interest tax deduction. As most know, interest paid on credit cards used to be tax deductible. With recent "tax reforms" this deduction was phased out. Let's bring it back, but in a different form: those who carry three cards during the tax year get to write off 50 percent of the interest paid; those who had two get to write off 75 percent, and those who only had one get a 100 percent writeoff, *plus* some kind of added incentive, maybe even a 50 percent bonus credit.

Next, put pressure on issuers. If a person already has three open universal card accounts, any account given to them over that number will be unenforceable in any court of law for collection purposes. How many consumers, especially those with very limited means, will then be showered with multiple cards by greedy issuers?

This seems preferable to directly interfering with interest rates (i.e. cost of money), and much more practical and to the point. Interest rates change all the time as the economy expands and contracts. Even tying interest rate incentives/regulations into some index (like the T-bill rate), might somehow interfere with an already sensitive, vulnerable economy.

This is not to say, however, that credit card interest rates should not be regulated. There must continue to be usury laws to keep such rates within an acceptable range. Anyone who might like to advance a 100 percent "free market" theory on this issue, i.e. "let demand dictate what the rate shall be," has to take into consideration the very real existence of loan sharking. We all know that loan sharking is and should continue to be illegal, yet tens of thousands of people continue to utilize this "service" on a daily basis. The vast majority of these citizens are the poor, the lower middle class, and the underclass/disenfranchised.

The trend has been and continues to be that we have institutionalized the universal card into a legal loan shark for the middle class. The analogy fits: If payments aren't made, a thug will not come to your house and break your arms and legs, but the issuer will not hesitate to wreak "economic violence" upon you in the form of wage garnishment and seizure of other assets. In any case, there are still threats and coercion. The simplest way to eliminate this is to do away with the processes which allow them to exist.

Taking the comparison a bit further, think about what those who use loan sharks borrow the money for: necessities such as chronicled above. More and more, *necessities* are being purchased on universal cards, especially food. That is why we must resolve to break this connection once and for all. If we do not, then we become economic slaves to the issuers, who have the power to "beat us up" financially and psychologically.

My own experiences with insolvency help prove this analogy. Each and every day a client or potential client tells me a little horror story about the collection tactics used by one of their creditors. While there are many federal and state laws regulating collection agencies, they still yield much power, and can make someone's life absolutely miserable.

"If I don't get a payment by Friday I'm gonna garnish your wages" is something a potential client of mine hears every day. As I tell them, the bill collector is conveniently leaving out all the steps necessary to effect actual wage garnishment: draft and serve lawsuit, prove case in court, obtain court judgment. Depending on how fast the creditor moves and whether or not the debtor answers or litigates the lawsuit, this process can take six months before a creditor gets the right to garnish (seize a portion of) someone's wages. Of course, problems with taxing authorities like the IRS are an entirely different matter; the tax levy process does *not* require a court judgment.

The debtor is yelled at, humiliated, intimidated, and threatened by bill collectors trying to get a payment, even if it's only $50. Many clients are puzzled about why the collector is going to so much trouble; the fact is that many of them receive a commission based on gross collections. Many bill collectors now work out of their homes through computer modem connections with their employers. As a result, they are not as well supervised as they are on the creditor's premises.

Tactics that are barely legal abound: one that is common is "verifying employment." While it is usually illegal to call a person's employer and say the debtor is a "deadbeat" and won't pay, the collector will repeatedly call payroll and ask to verify John Doe's employment there. They will then let it "slip out" that they are from "X" Bank and are "very concerned about John." The payroll folks, especially in a smaller company, quickly realize what is up, and may call John's supervisor or John himself, saying that John better get square on this debt so the harassment will stop.

Another tactic involves the use of special phone directories which list street addresses in numerical order, rather than by name. If a debtor ignores a collector's call or doesn't respond the way they would like, the next step can be a call to the target's neighbor: "Gee, this is Bob from X Bank. I've been trying to get a hold of John your neighbor about a 'personal' matter...have you seen him? If you do, will you tell him it's *urgent* that he call me right away to solve this 'problem'...."

Now Mr. Collector really hasn't called John's neighbor and said John is a deadbeat who doesn't pay his bills, has he? Yeah, right, as my seven-year-old says.

When John soon makes his way to my office he is embarrassed and angry at the way he was treated by the formerly "friendly" creditor. I'll usually say something like, "This is what happens when you make a deal with the devil...." I am not trying to make the person feel worse, but am attempting to guide them back to reality. Reality at this point is that when you accept a "preferred" card at a high rate of interest which is accepted without question almost anywhere, you must pay the monthly payment or be subject to such treatment.

So in a sense, we *have* institutionalized middle-class loan sharking. Completely legal and accepted, plastic cards can get a grip on us that is almost as strong as the neighborhood gangster. Again, the only difference is that you don't get *physically* beaten for noncompliance. Too remote? Bad analogy, you may say? I have heard other attorneys and bankers openly advocate a return to debtor's prisons for certain "economic crimes"! Why not just throw down the gauntlet and let thugs hit the delinquent debtor once or twice for each day the payment is late. If he or she is not hurt too badly they can still go to work the next day and earn money to pay this creditor and any others they may have. Maybe a black eye or two would set an example for other would-be deadbeats that they had better not stop making those monthly payments...

The other side of credit card problems is excessive credit limits. Too many people have unsecured credit lines on universal cards that if "maxed-out" or used in their entirety, couldn't be paid-off in less than twenty years at the person's current income level.

Again, as an advocate of individual rights, I believe that government should not directly regulate a "commodity," even a border-line one like this. However, there is nothing wrong with offering incentives or rewards to people for policing themselves.

As chronicled above, greedy issuers shower large unsecured lines upon those unable to fully repay. Just like multiple cards, excessive credit limits are an invitation to personal financial disaster. They can be as tempting and seductive as any of the many vices and dangerous things/behaviors which we routinely regulate.

The solutions here are similar to those suggested with multiple cards: tax incentives to consumers for keeping open unsecured credit lines within a certain range in the calendar year. The range should be a ratio based upon the individual or couple's taxable earnings for that particular year. For example, if a couple earns $50,000 and had open lines of credit under $10,000 (20 percent) that year, they might get a flat tax credit of $300-400 from Uncle Sam (you and me!). If their open credit exceeded the agreed-upon guideline, then they are not penalized, but just do not get the tax credit.

On the other hand, I believe that issuers/grantors, being in a superior financial position than that of the average consumer and possessing vast resources that enable them to make precise financial evaluations, *should* be penalized for overextending credit to someone. One solution would be to take away legal enforceability of credit card obligations after a certain dollar amount, based upon the person's income, is given out in new credit. This would be a great incentive for issuing institutions to communicate properly between themselves.

Instead of devoting data resources to simply "badmouthing" or trying to collect delinquent payments from a particular consumer, perhaps these entities will work together to see that a logical, common sense package of credit is granted. Perhaps there would then be more competition between granting entities for services they offer, and we would see *real* benefits instead of the usual lame ones like towing insurance.

In their quest for more paying customers in a limited market, perhaps grantors would institute credit counseling at the onset of usage *before* disaster strikes! What a novel concept! Imagine helping someone before they have to be harassed for payment or before they have to come see me about a bankruptcy. Could our society handle such positiveness all at once?

Didn't we do the same thing with the concept of "preventive medicine"? For decades much of the focus of American medicine was on treatment of the ill, especially through surgery. As we approach the 21st century there is more and more emphasis on prevention. What brought this about in the medical establishment? Many will argue that it was not benevolence, but economic pressure from ordinary citizens, insurance companies, businesses, and government, upon medical providers. In other words, "Tell us what we can do now to avoid six or seven figure cures in the future." Shouldn't we look at overspending problems in the same light? After our physical health, isn't financial health a priority item?

If we do not formally take such steps, who will? Should we follow the opinions of some and merely wait for a mysterious, omniscient "free market" to make adjustments for us? Or would such adjustments entail things we would not like, such as a second Depression, perhaps worse than the last?

Further regulations must be made concerning credit bureaus and the reporting of people's accounts. The present system stinks. A purported creditor can say it wants about a person's handling of that account. If the report is found later to be inaccurate (usually when the consumer is at the dealer trying to buy a car or is in the middle of escrow on a house), the person has the right to "dispute" the item with the credit bureau which then "investigates" by inquiring of the creditor. It can easily take several months to get an inaccurate report fixed.

The credit bureaus are all too eager (since federal law requires them) to tell you that if you still disagree with the creditor's report, you can add your own statement to your profile next to that creditor's.

Big deal. I have had bankers tell me that they just *laugh* at the consumer's explanation, giving it little or no credence—the *creditor's* report controls; pay up or go somewhere else. If the creditor says you paid 180 days late, then you did. If you'd like to spend your life savings suing a large bank or retailer for defamation, go ahead. I have many competent colleagues who would litigate your case for $10,000 or more as an initial retainer. (And they would deserve and earn such fees—big companies' defense attorneys will inundate plaintiffs with tons of paper that would have to be dealt with, requiring many hours of work.)

State and federal laws concerning credit bureaus should be changed (who do you think wrote them in the first place?!) to put the burden on the creditor making the report and the credit bureau itself to make sure the report is completely accurate. In law this concept is known as strict liability. If something wrong occurs, you must pay damages even if you weren't "negligent." Stiff fines and large civil penalties should be required for such infractions. Why so extreme?

Because credit is no longer a convenience, it is a requirement for modern American society. People with certain "black marks" on their credit can be shut down financially with a few strokes on the keyboard.

As discussed above, many necessary functions of the average consumer are now wholly dependent upon the utilization of a universal credit card. Obviously, if the account is shut down, so is the person's ability to transact.

Why must it be this way? Do we give credit grantors this power over us by default? Why not use a *subsystem* to take this power away?

Such a subsystem would be a nominal (like $2,000) credit line, guaranteed by a governmental entity but issued by a private bank just like student loans are. The great difference would be that this credit line would be available to *all* citizens with certain qualifications, and could *not* be arbitrarily taken away as is the case now. Administrative procedures and hearings would be required in order to terminate this "lifeline" account, similar to the steps which must be taken if a state wants to take away your driver's license. As more and more financial transactions require a universal credit card, then the wisdom of such a subsystem will become more apparent.

In sum, there would have to be changes and constraints on universal cards and their promulgation. The present system is weighted heavily against the average consumer. It is fraught with traps and pitfalls, and is structured to give unfair advantages to grantors and other institutions. The little guy is under a big thumb.

This country has always operated on the foundation of

personal freedom, a personal and collective work ethic, and the constitutionally guaranteed right to tell various tyrants to "take a hike."

We have created and continue to nurture certain economic tyrants within every aspect of our society. It is high time to de-claw these little monsters and attempt to regain our individual freedoms.

PREDICTIONS

There have been newspaper stories lately concerning a so-called "compulsiveness gene" which predisposes an individual to act in certain ways, under certain circumstances. I haven't seen much in the way of specifics on this issue, and even so, such matters are above my level of expertise.

From a logical and common sense point of view, it seems to me that we have a long way still to go in determining what is normal and abnormal behavior as far as human beings are concerned. Much of the time "normal" becomes what some authority or societal consensus decrees it to be.

Take for example again cigarette smoking. Once it was considered "normal" to smoke; now smoking is "abnormal." We say that people who smoke are "compulsive" because they do so in an addictive manner and cannot stop, even with overwhelming evidence of its deadly effects.

In a less physiological sense, take a socially unacceptable behavior like shoplifting. We hear about people who get arrested because they cannot stop themselves from pocketing merchandise whenever they go into a store. Often the merchandise is something they don't even need; they just repeat the behavior because they feel "compelled" to. This is labeled "abnormal" and in American society it is.

But there are groups and subcultures in other parts of the world today where stealing in this manner is not only accepted, but required. We view killing other people (unless sanctioned by the government in warfare or criminal executions) as "abnormal" and heinous. Yet in other societies, or even in our own American subcultures, it is desirable or required.

When these contradictions become apparent, it becomes harder to define what compulsiveness is. I remember debates among psychiatrists in the '70s about the very definition of mental illness. One theory of the day said that the people we label as "insane" are really "sane" individuals reacting to an insane world. This was prior to many of the discoveries about diseases like schizophrenia, which now seem clearly linked to a physical defect or genetic trigger mechanism/complex, rather than a purely behavioral response; i.e., a medical problem that creates certain behaviors.

When we talk about those who spend in such a way as to threaten their financial and physical survival and label them compulsive, and there appears to be a way to modify this behavior on a biological level, then there will be efforts to do so that I predict will dwarf present methods of behavioral control.

When I was in junior high school (1960s) we were told that little was known about the human brain. Thirty-something years later a little more is known, and we have seen whole sets of psychoactive compounds that alter consciousness and behavior, most of which are used to treat the "mentally ill."

More and more behaviors seem subject to direct control. It is logical to extrapolate present reality to a future where we can take a pill that will keep us from eating too much, taking illicit drugs, doing physical violence upon others, or spending into financial ruin.

If that becomes the case, then scores of new questions and

issues will demand answers: who decides what is acceptable or normal? When are certain behaviors okay to exhibit? What behaviors will be modified and by whom? Not only would the criminal justice system as we know it be altered beyond recognition, but so would the rest of society.

If we could take a pill and immediately trim or eliminate excesses like compulsive spending or spending above one's means, then new strategies will have to be developed to deal with subissues related to plastic or other forms of credit. Perhaps for the first time in human history borrowing as we know it will be eliminated, as everyone just uses what they have or takes only what they need.

I don't see all this occurring in the very near future.

One of the great "American traits" is competition, especially in business when similar products are developed and sold. In the last ten years we have seen new universal cards enter the marketplace, trying hard to get their piece of the pie. Now we have reached a point where almost every citizen either has one or will have one. Just like with long-distance phone service "carriers," they implore us to use their card instead of the other guy's.

I believe that a saturation point will soon be reached. Whenever the same service is offered to a large group of people, a shakeout eventually occurs. Arguably, the marketplace cannot infinitely sustain profits on the same type of service. With great technological leaps in data processing and communication, both time and space as we know it continue to "shrink." All trends point toward centralization: small family-owned farms become part of large corporate superfarms, small companies become a division of multinational corporations, banks merge with other banks, etc.

The present state of universal credit card use—many cards with varying limits being carried by the same person, seems ripe for consolidation. One card with all banking and credit functions seems more efficient for accounting purposes and other purposes as well. If a saturation point is reached where issuing entities can no longer make the profits they desire, then the next logical step would be consolidation. Already this concept seems to be in the works: issuers send mass mailings every day touting their "better interest or monthly payment rate," along with little preembossed checks so the consumer can "consolidate all those high-interest, large-payment accounts into one easy payment."

What I see is that eventually the average citizen will carry one multi-function card. This will give them access to all checking and investment accounts, their particular *total* line of credit, and will also allow a potential grantor or other entity one is doing some transaction with, to access set identifying data like: birth certificate, work history, medical history, credit profile, and even perhaps genealogy or genetic record. Not only would this eliminate the cost and inefficiency of carrying multiple types of identification and other descriptive records, it would make numerous verification steps obsolete.

This "service," the compilation, constant record updating, and electronic storage of data, will have to be done by some entity. In such a world, every citizen would have to utilize the services of this carrier just like with the long-distance phone companies.

I see a small group of carriers surviving future shakeouts to become America's choice for this service. They would not only be compilers, but also credit grantors and so would be the future version of what we know today as banks, savings and loans, credit unions, etc. Perhaps in the next 20-30 years we will see a "Big Three" emerge like we had with the largest American car manufacturers.

The structure of such entities would be quasigovernmental, like the post office, or perhaps a public entity. This would be proper because of the *necessity* of the entity's services and the level of *protection* of an individual's rights that will be required.

Today there is a plethora of data on every aspect of an individual's existence from womb to tomb. Data on a person starts being compiled even before they are conceived; there are sperm counts, genetic tests, sonograms, tests of amniotic fluid, then all the medical analysis during and after birth.

There is footprinting, fingerprinting, assignment of social security number, the various school-related processes, driving and other licensing, tax and earning records, etc. But all this information remains widely scattered. We already have the technology to have it complete in one place, so barring intentional efforts to the contrary, the day must come when it all will be.

At that point, individual freedom will be threatened like it has never been before. The entire "story" on a person will be available without using multiple reporting authorities. Less "doctoring" of records will be possible—it would become an "all or nothing" procedure.

Special laws, perhaps a constitutional amendment, would be necessary to define and enforce the rights each citizen has as they relate to this "core data." Everything we are or could be within society will depend upon what our "core data" says. Already we routinely see the powerful effects of data sharing: one who does not pay their student loans or child support has money seized from their tax refund or some other resource. Those who fail to buy auto insurance or register their vehicle have their driving privileges revoked. Criminals and those accused or suspected of crimes, are routinely tracked anywhere in the world through credit card records.

The development and eventual perfection of core data will make every individual's location and hundreds of other characteristics instantly accessible to those who are able to gain access. The potential for abuse is unlimited. Imagine the consequences if such data had been available to Hitler or

Stalin. In today's world, there are thousands of little Hitlers alive and in varying positions of power, both within governments at all levels and private enterprise of all kinds. The potential for worldwide fascism exists like never before. Only a carefully thought out system of core data protection, strictly enforced, can keep such horror from unfolding. Already there is research in progress on the human brain's electrical processes that could make mindreading as easy as looking at a computer screen.

In the 21st century, wealth will probably be measured by an individual's ability keep data about themselves private; "Knowledge is power" will be distilled into "Data on others and privacy regarding oneself is the ultimate power."

What started less than fifty years ago as a convenient way to acquire goods and services without immediate cash will evolve into the real possibility of complete control by others.

The natural evolution of the link between our bodies and "Core Data Central" will be the existence of some sort of implant within our bodies. Long a staple of science-fiction, the technology for such a thing is already present reality. In addition to eliminating the need to carry something, the device would also monitor the body's ongoing functions, perhaps becoming a necessity in the future practice of medicine. Just as having credit cards is now a major factor in separating "Haves" from "Have-nots" in American society, the future may also see the same type of demarcation regarding implants. Perhaps there will be different kinds of implants, with varying degrees of sophistication and "allowed privacy" available; a person's socioeconomic status is then determined by what kind of implant they have, much like automobile ownership used to be an indication thereof.

The more implants, the more core data sitting in Data Central. The "trick" will be to achieve the status of having great power through a better implant (more services, benefits available) but maintaining greater privacy (greater "wealth"). In this future the very mortality of a person's body will be dependent upon data that will enable doctors to detect a disease years before it makes its presence known, or be correlated with other data based on genetic history/present makeup, to change the aging/deterioration process.

In such a world the "Haves" will live longer in exchange for giving out more data about themselves. The disenfranchised or "Have-nots" may turn out to be those who will not or cannot compile and distribute as much data about their bodies, and therefore would have less chance of optimum medical monitoring and problem prevention, living less years. (Is this a whole lot different than today's world, where those with more and better resources like food and medicines tend to live longer than their counterparts who do not have such access?)

The economic "pecking order" is already well-defined: with some exception, today's "Haves" are those with the most credit, and usually can obtain as many universal credit cards and other unsecured lines of credit as they desire. When used in reference to the "middle class," the multiple universal card concept is more significant, since the "rich" (multimillionaires on up) do not have or need more than a few cards—they use universal cards more as a convenience than as an extension of income and assets, whereas those of the middle class down to the "underclass" use plastic as a straight extension of their incomes.

One of the great defining characteristics of someone in the underclass is a lack of credit, especially through universal credit cards. Such an individual finds himself completely excluded from performing routine economic functions that the majority takes for granted. This is akin to the lack of a checking account twenty to thirty years ago.

As core data becomes reality, the gap between socioeconomic classes will necessarily widen. I see a future where the underclass will consist of those unable to get a data implant, or perhaps forbidden to obtain more than a rudimentary one.

This would be analogous to someone in today's society who has no universal credit card, telephone, or vehicle—they still must function within society, but operate at a great economic disadvantage compared to other citizens—they have less, slower, and incomplete access to existing resources, and therefore have less material goods and other elements of what we currently define as "wealthy."

In the United States, there has always existed some sort of mechanism to help those designated as "disadvantaged"—from colonial church or community-sponsored helping hands, to vast governmental megaprograms (AFDC, Social Security) spending millions each day. The purported goal of such programs is "economic democracy"—bringing citizens in a lower socioeconomic group up to a level of sustenance where they can live a certain way—enough food to eat, shelter, clothing, and basic material goods. Many of these programs endeavor to put the individual or family in a position where they can grow and develop to a self-sustaining, producing member of society (higher class). Supposedly, once a certain level is reached, the person is more "equal" to other citizens: once certain minimum resources are obtained, other rights and privileges of citizenship become obtainable and exercisable.

As we have seen many times in world history, however, there seems to be a tendency of groups to have wider gaps between them than social planners might like: monarchy-peasant, rich-poor, etc. In most human societies the concept of "one or the other" seems more prevalent than the diamond-shaped model with small tops, bottoms, and a large middle. In 20th century America alone, the socioeconomic "shape" has shifted many times, and continues to change—it is not static, but always in motion.

Some economists posit that the end of the 1980s marked the beginning of a pattern which will mimic Depression times—a sunken middle class, with more people just rich or poor, like in 3rd world countries.

Of course, if "economic democracy" succeeds, then there would be only a small or nonexistent underclass, an upper (ruling) class, and a large middle class. The great difference then would be that our middle class citizens would be "better off" than the majority of upper-class citizens in other countries.

It is hard to extrapolate facts and predict what is going to occur economically in this country along with the rest of the world we are now so intertwined with.

On one end you have those predicting a worldwide economic collapse and depression; on the other you have those foreseeing a future of abundance for all.

As far as this country is concerned, I prefer to focus on its economic future in terms of smaller trends that could turn into larger realities, similar to what Toffler refers to as "Waves."

I see universal credit card usage increasing. More people will have them, more transactions will require them, all for the reasons economist Kamin gave. Prior to the "core data" implants I see today's universal card evolving into, there will be numerous stages that the "system" will go through.

Now we are seeing the emergence of universal cards with little economic "shifts" like rebates and discounts. Once such services gain a foothold, people will be ripe for diversity of function: "What can you do for me now?" Assuming no economic collapse in the immediate future, I see a shakeout coming in universal cards—many issuers will do something else with their capital as a saturation point is reached. As citizens become more aware of the evils of high interest rates, they will demand and get decreases in what issuers charge. I see this coming about through the forces of supply and demand at work in the marketplace and direct government regulations. This lessening of profit and potential profit will accelerate the aforementioned shakeout.

As more people acquire universal cards, especially in multiples, the bankruptcy filings should increase in the long term. I believe this because the concept of a "credit card bankruptcy" as exhaustively detailed above is new to the bankruptcy laws and the length of time the cards themselves have been in widespread use. So there will be two trends unfolding at the same time—a decrease in the number of issuers, along with lower interest rates and more functions available to the holder-consumer. Then, more personal bankruptcies as the process works its course.

The future of the bankruptcy laws themselves is still to be decided. There is a growing perception by those working in the field and the general public that changes are needed. A mere five years ago I was shocked when someone who owed 40-50 thousand dollars on universal cards came to me for a consultation. In 1993 alone I spoke with or filed cases for more than fifty individuals or married couples with universal card debt over $70 thousand, most of which exceeded the $100,000 mark!

One would think that, faced with such monumental losses, the issuers would bring such a granting process to a screeching halt, but I have seen no evidence of this. If anything, I have seen a *decrease* in the number of adversary complaints (when a creditor asks the judge to allow its debt to survive the bankruptcy) from a couple of years ago. This of course is not empirical evidence—perhaps my fine reputation alone deters issuers from filing such actions. More likely is that they have shifted their strategy and capital into other arenas.

Specifically, they have learned that the bankruptcy laws

will not protect issuers after they indiscriminately give multiple cards and high credit lines to people who are clearly unqualified to have them. There are some bankruptcy judges who will not hold a debtor liable for *any* charges made on an unsolicited account. The creditors' lobby is powerful—today they are working very hard for changes in the law, trying to make discharge in bankruptcy tougher.

I predict that this will also fail. The core principle of bankruptcy has always been and always will be the concept of a "fresh start." This idea is deeply ingrained within and flows directly from the Judeo-Christian concept of "absolution" (i.e. from "sin," "mistakes"). I believe that this is so much a part of our cultural infrastructure that attempts to abolish or gut the bankruptcy fresh start will be unsuccessful.

If this turns out to be accurate, and my other predictions become reality, then we will be well along the road to "one person, one card," in implant form, as described above.

By 1998 we will see that one of two large or "megatrends" has occurred: 1.) The national economy has taken a great turn for the better and mimics the '80s in many ways; or 2.) The national economy has deteriorated to a point where inflation is high, interest rates are high, and few consumers are given *any* new credit lines.

It is this span, 1995–1998, that should tell us what will happen to our nation's economy for the next twenty years, and how quickly today's universal credit card will evolve into the universal implant. It will show us which of the surviving issuing entities will become a future "carrier" for an individual's core data.

I see this as a period of great upheaval in the U.S., much like the late 1960s, but faster and more intensified. In the late '60s, the "Data Superhighway" we now hear about each day was just a dirt road. The paving is still going on; by 1996-97 traffic will be whizzing by at top speed. All citizens will be simultaneously wired to each other in many different ways. The flow of information will be immediate. Individuals will have less time to react to unfolding events than in the past, directly affecting group behavior.

We remember the '60s because so many changes took place in a very short period of time and different groups of people simultaneously reacted in new ways. We will look back upon the '90s as a supercharged version of this, with many more changes. The old adage "knowledge is power" will be underscored. The collection, interpretation, and use of raw data will be more directly related to "wealth" than ever before. Those who can interpret and utilize the great amounts of data in the most efficient and profitable ways will accumulate wealth faster than others. Proof of this already exists if we look at the example of computer software.

Once the technology for personal computers was perfected and millions of units were manufactured and sold, the demand for software to make them do things exploded. Those who knew how to write programs for desired uses quickly became extremely wealthy (e.g. Bill Gates) in a very short period of time. Contrast this with the number of years it took someone like John D. Rockefeller to accumulate comparable wealth in another era.

And so it will be on the sociological level. As information and ideas spread instantly, they will be put into effect almost immediately or will be rejected just as swiftly. This will accelerate changes in every part of society. We will see things happen in hours or days that used to take months or years to unfold in the past.

The leading example of this is the overthrow of communism in the former Soviet Union—it took place over a period of *days* in the '90s; the Russian Revolution in the early part of this century, though earmarked for convenience at 1917, actually took place over a period of years.

There will be hundreds of little revolutions in America between now and the turn of the century. Politicians, bureaucrats, and business leaders will come and go, along with their ideas, at a dizzying pace. The world of the Industrial Revolution will finally give way to the "Third Wave" predicted by Toffler.

One thing that remains constant is the physical structure of the human brain and the rest of the body. People will in effect be constantly "reprogrammed" as change accelerates. We will face unprecedented mental, physical, and emotional stress as individuals, which will then be manifested in group behavior. Already we see fast changes in stress-related behaviors—violence, substance abuse, and other compulsion-related activities.

Therefore, it is reasonable to predict more extreme behaviors regarding spending on credit. There will be more bankruptcies in a shorter time because the actions which led to it are simplified and accelerated.

There will be a period of years before the core data implant becomes universal, where we will see the final peak of massive overspending on credit. After that there will be more external controls in place. However, these "controls," no matter what form they end up taking, will not be a cure for all overspending/overextension problems. The only true control is self-control; we must be responsible for and be prepared to control our own financial destinies as the pace picks up and these changes take effect.

If we do not, then outside forces will be waiting, all too eager to do it for us. The result can only be less personal freedom and subjugation to the underclass of the future.

2010: A Middle-class American

Ralph still had twenty minutes before it was time to leave for work. He decided to skip the news and check his finances instead. Payday was almost a week away, and it was important to keep within budget.

He sat down in his favorite easy chair and gave a verbal command. The wall now contained a four-foot high screen.

"General checking, please."

"You have one thousand new dollars left in this account," the voice answered. Ralph knew this was just enough for one week's groceries and a night out.

"Bills payable next ten days, please."

"Your consolidated utilities bill is due on the tenth in the amount of one thousand two hundred new dollars; your car payment in the amount of two thousand five hundred new dollars is due on the twelfth…"

"Hmm, available credit, please."

"Your Megabank credit line is in the amount of one hundred thousand new dollars, of which eighty thousand new dollars is currently available."

"Okay, access current South Pole Adventure Vacation packages please."

An Underclass American

Jake drummed his fingers on the chair arm as the voice answered, "Two years, twenty-one days left until you may reapply to Megabank. Your U.S. government lifeline credit is in the amount of twelve thousand five hundred new dollars, of which three thousand new dollars is currently available."

"Hmmm…access tomorrow's program at Freehold Raceway, please."

Bibliography

Buttenheim, Alison; Buri, Sherri. "College Costs: The Pizza Factor: Here's How to Help College Students Stay One Step Ahead of the Bill Collectors—And What to Do If They Don't," *Changing Times*, January, 1990.

Cramer, James. "Card Sharks: The MasterCard Bandits," *New republic*, October 26, 1992.

Faber, Ronald. "Money Changes Everything: Compulsive Buying from a Biopsychosocial Perspective." *American Behavioral Scientist*, July-August 1992, p. 809.

Feinberg, Richard. "Credit Cards as Spending Facilitating Stimuli: A Conditioning Interpretation." *Journal of Consumer Research*. December 1986, p. 348.

Galanoy, Terry. *Charge It*. Putnam, 1980.

Holder, Ted. "The Japanese Discover the Perils of Plastic." *Business Week*, February 10, 1992.

Iida, Jeanne. "Visa Sees Huge Loss in Bankruptcy Frauds," *American Banker*, September 15, 1992.

Mandell, Lewis. *Credit Card Use in the United States*. Ann Arbor, Michigan: Institute for Social Research, 1972.

Mathews, H. Lee; Solcum, John W., Jr. "Social Class and Commercial Bank Credit Card Usage," *Journal of Marketing*, January 1969, p. 71.

Matthews, Arlene. *The Psychology of Money*, Krieger Publishing, 1991.

Meehan, John. "Past Due! The Bill for Consumer Debt Arrives," *Business Week*, December 10, 1990.

O'Guinn and Ronald Faber. "Compulsive Buying: A Phenomenological Exploration," *Journal of Consumer Research*, September 1989, p. 147.

Von Hostitz, Glenn; Alcamo, Michael. "Plastic, Fantastic Profits: A Troubled Bank Puts It All on the Card and Cardholders," *Harper's Magazine*, August, 1991.